THE TEACHINGS OF OSCAR CAMILLE

VOLUME I

THE TEACHINGS OF
OSCAR CAMILLE

Volume I

Paul Edward Napora

Blue Dolphin Publishing

Published by Blue Dolphin Publishing, Inc.
P.O. Box 8, Nevada City, CA 95959
Orders: 1-800-643-0765

ISBN: 0-931892-36-8

Library of Congress Cataloging-in-Publication Data

Camille, Oscar (Spirit)
   The teachings of Oscar Camille / [channeled by]
   Paul Edward Napora
      p.   cm.
   ISBN 0-931892-36-8 (v. 1). — ISBN 0-931892-37-6 (v. 2)
   1. Spirit writings.   2. Spiritual life—Miscellanea.   I. Napora,
   Paul Edward, 1939–   . II. Title.
   BF1301.C34   1996
   133.9'3—dc20   96-8154
                                                          CIP

Printed in the United States of America by
Blue Dolphin Press, Inc., Grass Valley, California

5   4   3   2   1

Contents

Dedication

I humbly dedicate this book to the past, to the present, and to the future.

Introduction

IT IS SINCERELY HOPED that this book will guide you, will enlighten you, and will teach you the way to greater pastures and calmer waters in life. The pain and hardships on earth can be excruciating at times, but, now and again, God sends a helping hand to those who seek and to those who are inspired by Him and His plans for life.

Over the years, Oscar, my Guardian Angel, has also guided and inspired me. He has never failed me nor hundreds of other people over the years. I am humbly grateful to be alive on earth and to be able to share his insights, his knowledge, and his wisdom with you.

As you read this book, always strive to remember that it was inspirationally written with my Guardian Angel, Oscar Camille, whom I assure you is very much alive and well. He is extremely kind, gentle, and soft-spoken. To serve mankind is to also serve God—and this, my dearest reader, is what this book is all about.

I wish you well, as does my guide, Oscar Camille—for wherever this book may wander or roam, we will be there too. May God bless you and keep you in happiness, peace, and prosperity, now and forevermore.

Paul Edward Napora

1

Who Is Oscar Camille?

Oscar Camille is a Cosmic Master. He is my Guardian Angel who was assigned to me at birth. Over the years I have come to know him not only as a personal friend, but as a loyal ally in times of great stress and need. He is always there when I need him—just as your "guide" or Guardian Angel is always there for you.

My story begins in 1939 about a month before my birth. My mother, Annie, fainted and in her faint saw a beautiful stairway leading to the sky. At the top of the stairway was a door. She knelt down, and the door opened. Mom says that Jesus was standing at the top of the stairway, and He asked her whether she wished to "come now or later." Mom answered that she wanted to return for her family's sake. Jesus said, "Very well." The next thing Mom saw was "the brightness of the sun" coming right through her. Shortly after this experience, she heard my father, Paul, trying to revive her. He did so, and an ambulance was called and rushed her to the hospital where she remained for two weeks. Two weeks later, on October 26, in Vegreville, Alberta, I was born at home with the assistance of two midwives.

I remember being at my grandmother's house on a farm near Beauvallon, Alberta, when I was five years old. I remember the following strange event as though it had taken place yesterday. I would go to sleep, and, each night for a week, I would experience this strange "dream." I could see myself sitting at a small table on whose center rested a large, white candle. Then, seven men dressed in the purest white, hooded robes would sit around this table and commence to decide my fate. I could not distinguish their faces because of the hoods which covered their heads—their faces were not shown to me at all. Although these men were wise, kind, and very pleasant, I was still a bit nervous, being a child of only five years. I can recall one of the men saying, "He is the one we want." However, another would interject, "I am not sure he will fulfill those tasks set out before him." This scenario went on and on each night in my dreams for a week. On the last night of the dream, all the men voted unanimously that I was "the one," supposedly chosen to carry out some special task(s) or mission(s) in life. Who knows? Perhaps this book is just one of those tasks or missions in my life—time will tell.

My parents used to own a poolroom in Vegreville. I can recall coming home from school one day in 1949, when I was nine years old. As I was walking by the downtown theater with some books in my hands, I was completely dumbfounded and immobilized by hearing a man's voice in my right prophetic ear state, "Your father has passed on." I began to cry and quickly ran to the poolroom where I thought my mother would be. She was there, alone. I ran to her, hugged her tightly, and shouted, "Daddy's dead! Daddy's dead!" With tears in her eyes, Mom asked me how I knew. I immediately said, "My angel told me so!" My father had died earlier that very afternoon of a massive heart attack. I shall never forget this experience as long as I live.

My next "psychic" experience took place when I was eleven years old. I was alone at home on a beautiful Sunday afternoon. My brother, Alex, had left a piece of paper and a pencil on the kitchen table. I was reading a book when suddenly I heard a man's voice shout in my right ear, three times, "Write! Write! Write!" I was literally guided to the table and began to feverishly write poetry. This marked the beginning of my writing career.

My first manuscript, "Poems and Passion," was completed when I was fourteen. I certainly thought it was ready to be published and submitted this script to a publisher or two but without success. When I was seventeen, I decided to revise my work a little bit here and there, and wait for an opportune moment to submit it to another publisher.

At age eighteen, I moved to Edmonton, Alberta, and found a job with a national telecommunications company. About a year later, my sister, Mary, told me about a "famous medium" with whom she had an appointment. The medium's name was Mrs. Louisa Rae, from Edinburgh, Scotland. Mary did go see her and was very impressed with her "spiritual reading." I made an appointment to go see Mrs. Rae—and it was at this time of my life, at nineteen, that my road in life became more clearly defined.

I went to where Mrs. Louisa Rae was staying. Her assistant, Mr. Brown, answered the door, looked at me calmly, and ushered me to where she was sitting. Immediately upon seeing me, Mrs. Rae covered her eyes with her arm as though she couldn't bear to look. "My child," she said, in a kindly and soft-spoken way, "I cannot bear to look at you, for you are as bright as the sun." Confused, I thought, "What is she saying—I am not her son!" She then uncovered her eyes, stared at me for a moment or two, and went on, "You know, we were told to come to Canada by our spirit guides, but we didn't know why." She kept staring at me, smiled, and then said, "Paul, I think you are our reason for coming here." I was rather flattered by her statement, but still I had no idea what this "reason" might be. Mrs. Rae got up, ushered me into a small room, and went into trance.

It is so difficult to fully describe in words what then transpired. Mrs. Rae's own voice was normally soft, feminine, totally recognizable as belonging to a woman. Yet, in her trance, the voices that came through her were undeniably, without any possibility of a doubt, unquestionably male! Seven angels came through Mrs. Rae in her "trance state." These seven angels knew more about me than I did myself! They knew things about me that only God and I could possibly have known. They mapped out my life so prophetically—even up to this very moment. I did not bring a recorder at that time, not knowing what to expect, so I was very preoccupied with jotting down information. (No doubt a recorder would have failed to function because of the tremendous amount of "power" in that room.) I recall one of the angels saying, "You are a writer. You have a manuscript now completed. Please wait for eight months before submitting this project south of the border." I now know this angel was Oscar.

At one point during this experience, Mrs. Rae introduced me to Oscar, my guide. She did not give me his last name; I was to find it out for myself much later. Oscar called me by my spiritual name, "Manuana," not my given name, Paul. This whole session lasted about one hour. Then Mrs. Rae came out of her trance, kindly offered me tea, and asked me to join her "circle group" in Edmonton. I was pleased to hear that she would be remaining in Edmonton for about a year, so I gratefully accepted her invitation. Mrs. Rae intimated that she could not leave Canada until her "mission" was accomplished.

There were about fifteen people in this circle group, including my sister, Mary, and we all faithfully met once a week in the basement of the Spiritualist Church in Edmonton. It was a mixed group of people—young, old—but all who attended seemed sincere in their efforts to "give of themselves" through silent meditation. Six months later, Mrs. Rae sprained her foot. Unable to join us for quite some time, she left Mr. Brown, her assistant, in charge of the meetings. The first day she could not attend, we were all saddened by her absence, because whenever she went into a trance, it became the highlight of the evening. It certainly was for me. Well, midway through our sitting, I began to feel "someone" push my head forwards, then backwards, then sideways, and all around. My hands were lifted, and my feet were prodded back and forth as though I were walking, sitting on my chair. Then suddenly, I blacked out! The next thing I recall was walking around the circle making blessing signs of a cross to everyone there and then blacking out again—and apparently giving "messages of high order" to everyone within the circle. Much later, I found myself seated once more in my chair, exhilarated yet a bit confused. I had unexpectedly, but obviously, gone into trance and literally took over where Mrs. Rae had left off. Oscar had at last come through me and used me for a rich, wholesome experience, which I shall never forget. My "third eye" was at last open!

When Mrs. Rae heard the good news, she was delighted. Her mission obviously was accomplished. The circle group continued for several months more; then she and Mr. Brown returned to Scotland.

Several months later, my sister and I went to visit a man-and-wife team, famous mediums in their own right. Mr. and Mrs. Claude Lister lived near Fort Saskatchewan, Alberta, at that time. Somehow, I wanted to be "tested" by them to be sure that my newly discovered "talents" were right on track, so to speak. Mr. Lister did test me, and I can recall him saying, "Paul, you have it. Use it wisely!"

It was during this period that I submitted my manuscript, "Poems and Passion," over the border to the Naylor Company in San Antonio, Texas. A contract arrived in the mail a month later. I cannot even begin to describe my feelings where my writing was concerned. It was a joy within a joy! At last my work was going to be published. *Poems and Passion* was published in 1961 and was followed by four other books: *The Cresset, Hiroshima, Auschwitz,* and *Death at Belsen*.

Oscar assigned me to meditate at certain times, after my first book was published. I would meditate by myself, and he would teach me the things I needed to know. Oscar would stand at a distance from me, and symbolically, I could see tiny lights tossed from him into my "third eye," located at the center bottom of my forehead. I continued to receive symbolic knowledge from him for several years. He once stated, "Manuana, you are actually attending 'University' from *this* side of life, and I am your mentor." Who was I to argue? I recognized his profound wisdom, though this did not stop me from testing him in various ways, only to have things backfire on me time and time again—in the form of truth. I realized then that he was wiser than I could ever be and gratefully accepted the fact. Eight years later, this basic training and testing period with Oscar was over. He felt I had met all the requirements necessary to carry on in my psychic endeavors.

On the last day of this period, Oscar came to me, holding a large, golden key in his hands. He said, "Manuana, I come to you with this golden key. You shall unlock many treasures and hidden secrets for your fellowman." He then moved closer and closer to me until he actually came right through me with the key.

Oscar Camille is back from the fourth century. He was born in France, and at an early age, he decided to become a monk. He eventually went to Tibet, where he did accomplish this mission, and died on this earth plane at the age of fifty-six.

Throughout my long association with Oscar, I have only been privileged to see his head, hands, feet, and a portion of his robe. He stands about 5′9″ and has a light complexion and a dark, grey beard. His voice is deep yet gentle, kindly yet stern, and always full of inner love.

Oscar has intimated to me that it takes about one thousand earth years to become a Guardian Angel. Some souls, however, being more advanced and privileged because of their love towards God and their fellowman, advance more readily on the other side. Life in the spirit world is constantly busy—that is, if the souls wish to progress and advance. All males on this earth plane have a male Guardian Angel with several fledgling guides behind him, who can be male or female; all females on this earth plane have a female Guardian Angel with several fledgling guides behind her, who can, as well, be male or female. All individuals on this earth plane have a spiritual name assigned to them from the other side of life. To discover this spiritual name, one must be properly attuned to the "higher Masters" on the other side of life. Most people, however, do not know their spiritual names until they reach the hereafter.

As this book is being written, Oscar will be communicating with me directly through my right prophetic ear and/or symbolically. The symbols that will be appearing to me look like hieroglyphics, which I am able to decipher and interpret instantly. I assume also, since this is the case very often, that I will be seeing clear and concise visions from time to time to clarify matters, if the need arises.

Let us now use that golden key to unlock some of those doors, discover some of those treasures, and share some of those precious secrets of Life that Oscar so eloquently expounded to me then—as he continues to do even now.

2

Life

Whether you are rich or poor, life on this earth plane is no easy task. There are moments, hours, or days when things appear to be going right, but, by the same token, there are just as many moments, hours, or days when matters within and around a person go sour. It is so true: nobody promised anyone a bed of roses! You have to work very hard to achieve those goals or aims set before you. There is no magic wand to happiness or success. You must willingly earn it, one way or another.

MANUANA, your earth plane is one centered upon experience, learning, and procreation. How could a person possibly learn anything without some form of struggle and pain? In the deepest valley the stars are, indeed, the brightest—so a person must organize his life's thoughts and actions accordingly and commence to visualize the positive and good aspects within and around him. What good can come from musing over the trials and tribulations already experienced? That field has already been plowed; do not look back. It is futile to moan or groan over one's struggles! Always strive to look ahead, and forge ahead with the inner intuitive knowledge embedded within you. Believe in God, bring out the Christ Light that is within you, and, indeed, you will prosper beyond your wildest imagination!

But, remember, as well, that no one on this earth planet is totally content or totally successful in all matters. Both the wisest and the lowly experience a lifetime of happiness and pain as they gently forge ahead. Life itself is to be experienced, and it is basically the positive aspects along your life's journey that will allow your heart, mind, and soul to grow. Always strive to remember, as well, that it is your soul that has its eternal roots with God. Consider beautiful experiences in your life as being a field of flowers you have gathered; consider your negative experiences as being a field of weeds you have plucked out.

Over the years I have met so many people who want to know more about man's origin, his journey, and his destination. Civilizations have come and gone, apparently leaving some monumental traces of man's mighty powers and expertise; yet, some destructive force or his own pride and wickedness annihilated him! It seems that man can go so far on this earth plane, and then out of the blue, something happens to wipe him off the face of this planet. Then, sadly, those remaining must start all over again. Old discoveries then become new discoveries many centuries later, or what man knew then must be rediscovered now, and so forth. Will peace come; will our present civilization survive?

Your Earth experiences many cycles both good and bad, whether these be man-created or created by the planet itself. Nothing on your world was meant to last forever nor will this be the case. Man was essentially "seeded" by the gods or, to update this fact, by the celestials from distant star systems. Ancient civilizations were not exactly as knowledgeable about star systems as your present civilization is. Man must and will colonize other planets in time, but first he must become attuned to the "higher frequencies" both within and around him. Although ancient civilizations have come and gone, you must remember that they did much good in their own way and did pave the way for others to follow.

Consider an ancient civilization as being basically at the bottom of a ladder. It climbed a step or two in order to fulfill its destiny. Each civilization climbs a step or two upon its evolutionary pathway in life. But bear in mind, as well, that both man and planet Earth itself can be very unpredictable.

Man makes his countless mistakes—and planet Earth can have its earthquakes, mud slides, and north and south pole variations. Never in the total history of man has a civilization such as the one you are presently abiding in made such quantum strides to seek and explore other worlds. Your civilization, at long last, is making the right efforts and strides to explore outer space. Man's mind has been "programmed" by the gods or celestials of ancient time to fulfill his rightful heritage—to be as a god or as a celestial in his own right. The brainpower in man today is much more gifted and, let us say, much wiser than that of ancient times. Actually, your civilization today is slowly entering the Space Age realities and is heading into the right territories where these matters are concerned.

However, many people around your world are not striving to improve upon their inner light through meditation and prayer. People meditate and merely think about themselves in the process, or they pray and merely ask for themselves instead of giving and sharing with their fellowman. Love your fellowman always! This alone is the ultimate key to a better existence on this side of life, Manuana. In many respects people do a lot of preaching, but they fail to adhere to their own good concepts and intuitive powers in life. They do not practice what they preach, so to speak. Man must learn to be at peace with himself and with his fellowman. The corruptions and abominations on your Earth planet today are not, by any means, wholesome or worthy of mention. Man can, however, change, but he must be willing to rekindle the Love of God within his being, rather than constantly thinking about money. He concentrates far too much upon materialistic gains rather than soul gains on this earth plane. This will never do!

As you already know, Manuana, no earthly government has ever stood the test of time; God's government, however, does! It does seem inevitable, however, that a "Higher Intercession" must weed the bad from the good—and thus, in truth, the meek will, at long last, inherit the earth. If all peoples of your planet would strive to work together, rather than foolishly living by some antichrist doctrines and laws, there would be that ultimate peace many people around your world seek. All countries should be working side by side in brotherhood and harmony so that the bonds of love become one. Unfortunately, many countries around your world are playing a cat-and-mouse game with each other. They are not looking through the Eyes of God; they are looking through the eyes of evil.

Happily, though, Manuana, your world will change in the future—but not before some prophecies of old are fulfilled. The Messiah, the King of Light, will return, and then, at last, your world will finally know peace and will finally join the Federated Planets of other worlds in distant universes beyond your earth plane. Yes, your present civilization will survive but not until the negatives are totally weeded out—and they will be!

Most people on earth have always had the impression that they have a "free will," or that they can actually alter their destiny through concerted actions, determination, prayer, meditation, and so forth. Is this true? Can man, as a whole, alter his destiny, or is life like a play in which everyone is a player acting out a part?

Certainly one's destiny can be altered, but the person involved must be willing to work very hard to make those alterations. Far too often, people become lazy and complacent in their earthly minds and actions, and simply do not bother to make matters better both within and around them. Manuana, you have heard that old saying, "God helps those who help themselves." Well, in essence, this is applicable to those who wish to alter or make improvements in their daily lives. People put themselves in an earthly quandary or rut, and fail to realize the importance of actually "picking themselves up and starting all over again." Unfortunately, they can stay in their sad state until the stars cease to shine, but this will not bring them any closer to changing their destiny. People who change their destiny are those willing to make personal sacrifices and attitudinal changes within their lives. If they do, then truly, they have altered their destiny path. Things become better, not worse!

Man can also change his destiny but, at the moment, is unwilling to look God in the eye and say, "All right, Father, I will change; I will work hand in hand with my fellowman; I will share my toil with others around me; I will pray for others; and I will strive wholeheartedly against greed and pride on earth." So essentially, when man dispels his hatreds, greed, and pride, it is at this juncture that his destiny can and will be altered. The best advice here is for each individual on earth to strive to be one's highest, purest self so that, in essence, one's destiny can be altered to a higher plateau, to a greater inner light, and to a more meaningful purpose of life not experienced before.

Many people have asked me about the miracle of birth, and whether or not the soul is present at the precise moment of conception. Also, topics such as miscarriage, abortion, and birth control are at the forefront of many people's minds on earth. What is precisely right and what is precisely wrong in man's ideas or concepts about these matters?

A soul is "assigned" to a seed. That seed is life. At the moment of conception the soul enters that seed. The seed grows and so does the soul. Both are pure and holy! In the event of a miscarriage, the soul must gently find its way to its Heavenly Mansion, where it will grow and prosper. In the event of an abortion, the soul must also find its way gently to its Heavenly Mansion, where it will grow and prosper. In the event of a miscarriage, God's Will is done. In the event of an abortion, man's will attempts to supersede God's. You must understand, as well, that there are many, many varying circumstances involving abortion. God sees these actions of abortion on earth and will judge those responsible accordingly, when they enter their designated mansion on this side of life. Nothing—absolutely nothing—goes unseen by God. Some people on your planet may pretend or fantasize that everything is all right after they have committed some wrongdoing, but believe me, there is a time and a place where souls are judged. Asking for forgiveness and feeling God's forgiveness within you are true signs that He has forgiven you. But if a person is forgiven and continues to harbor guilt feelings over the wrongdoing, then truly that person has rejected God's Forgiveness.

When a person is forgiven by God, he or she must strive very hard not to repeat the action and not to rekindle guilt over what was done. You know that old saying—forgive and forget! Well, God also forgives and forgets, providing the person involved believes this spiritual truth.

As for birth control, Manuana, this practice is essential on earth. Each person is a sexual being, as you and millions of other people on earth know, so it is totally logical to use birth control as needed or required. Sadly, many religions on your planet have bent the truth in some of these matters to suit their needs or to try to suppress their followers with antiquated fears, ideas, and ideals.

Oscar, can we talk about the children of this world and what the future might hold for them? There are so many conflicts created between parent and child nowadays, it is most difficult to fathom why this is so prevalent. There should be more love, harmony, and appreciation from the parent to the child and from the child to the parent, but there are many distinguishable "rifts" and "discord" in family upbringing in these changing times.

First of all, Manuana, many parents on this planet fail to realize that their children are not *their* children, but that all life belongs to God. Parents should always love, guide, and protect their children but should not assume that they can control the eventual independence of their children. There is not a person on this planet who can honestly say, "I own this" or "I own that." They do not *own* anything, actually, because everything is merely loaned to all life on your planet! Children are borrowed just as you or anyone else on this planet is loaned to his or her parents. Everything and everyone on planet Earth belongs to God.

Far too often parents feel that anything and everything they do on earth must be or should be carried on by their children. They fail to realize that their children are of God and that these children must also find their niche or road in life. You know that no two people are alike on this earth plane, Manuana; however, many parents fail to realize that their children are not exact carbon copies of themselves. The possessiveness, greed, hate, and other frustrations the parent may tend to harbor about life should be dispelled in order to properly bring up their family as sensible, earthly guardians. The inner frustrations some parents hold towards themselves, their offspring, and life in general can be most damaging, not only to their present earthly existence, but to their eternal souls as well. The problem lies with those responsible not seeking earthly and spiritual help. When two people get married, they should always vow to have the Christ Light in front of them, no matter how wonderful or distasteful life may be. In rearing their family, they should always treat those whom they love in a respectful, kindly, and, of course, loving manner. Many parents fail to reach out to God for the inner guidance they need; hence, their children suffer in the process.

And, of course, when their children suffer, Manuana, then a chain reaction commences. Their children's children often go through the same process. Ignorance, however, is no excuse! The minds and habits of anyone can change if that person is willing to change. Those beings who mistreat others on your earth plane do have a rude awakening on this side of life. They may say, "I did not know," or "I tried," or "I assumed that's how it should be," and so forth—but the truth is simple: You cannot deceive God's Light, no matter how hard you try! Many people, upon passing to this side of life, Manuana, are, in fact, put in a "psychological plane" until they realize, beyond any shadow of a doubt, that their wrongs did not create a right.

My advice to anyone on this earth plane is this: if you know better, then act accordingly. Do not get carried away with bitterness, hatreds, and vendettas that can lead to immeasurable trouble down the road of life. All children of your planet should be guided, protected, and loved the way God intended this to be—not the way man intends it to be. Pitiful is the soul who acts against God's Will; pitiful is the soul who misuses the gift of life in an uncaring, superficial, and prideful manner.

Your world will find its peace, Manuana, but not until some prophecies of old are fulfilled—and then, at long last, children will find their rightful place, peace, and comfort that they were always meant to have.

What about the "unfortunate ones," Oscar? Those beings who are born crippled, blind, diseased, retarded, or even insane. Why must they suffer? What wrong did they commit? What is their true place and purpose here on earth?

Manuana, a child that is born to your planet may be considered angelic in more ways than one. Children are, in fact, the purest form of life given to man. Some children are born whole and healthy; yet some are born, as you say, crippled, blind, diseased, retarded, or even insane. Why? Well, it is man's mission to procreate, but, in the act of procreation, in some cases the seed itself is not genetically programmed properly; thus, an offspring is born with weaknesses and instability. There are many other factors as well, Manuana. The so-called drug abuser, alcoholic parent, or diseased parent can produce an offspring with weaknesses and instability just as well. Nonetheless, these children are still children of God and must be loved and respected as well as possible. These children have committed no wrong—but those who are healthy, wealthy, and wise should be grateful for all their earthly blessings. Unfortunately, some people are not! Eventually, when these infirm children or adults pass on to this side of life, they become totally whole and healthy. The crippled will walk; the blind will see; the diseases will disappear; the retarded will think and act on their own; and, lastly, the so-called insane will awaken to their better mind and judgments on this side of life.

In the meantime, man must not ignore his true mission on earth—that is, to love his fellowman, whether he be healthy or unhealthy. It is the responsibility of the healthy individual to look after those considered less fortunate than himself. But also, do not overlook the inner gifts within some of those born with weaknesses and instability. Many crippled people on your planet do a lot more than those who can move around freely; many blind people have a greater insight than those who can see; many retarded people have talents and special abilities not given to those who can think and act clearly; and, lastly, many insane people are cured with major breakthroughs in science and psychology and can thus lead normal lives.

All Life is a miracle, and it is the mission of all Life to partake in the process assigned to it. Whether you are rich, poor, healthy, or unhealthy, there is a purpose and a plan for your existence. Suffering is a state of mind or brief passage on earth that should enrich the soul in humility. Without humility, there can be no passage available to any soul who longs for Heaven.

Oscar, what about human suffering as a whole—the wars, starvation, the evil injustices that take place in various countries, and so forth? It seems such a shame, such an unholy waste of time, that man with his so-called intelligence fails to realize that greed and power lead, in the end, to a total no-win situation!

Your world is a world of plenty and may be considered a literal Garden of Eden, if those who attempt to control it would realize this fact. There are many good countries on your planet that truly strive very hard to help those less fortunate beings in various poorer countries. However, many of these poorer countries are controlled by demagogues or dictators who are in league with the antichrist conceptions of life. Some of the so-called help received never actually reaches the intended needy and starving peoples. Their own government uses and abuses this help in ruthless, meaningless ways, such as buying armaments instead of helping and feeding its people.

And, as you already know, Manuana, there are many anti-christ groups and leagues present on your earth plane. The weak, suffering people constantly fear their dictatorship and are unable to break away from the stranglehold their government has imposed upon them.

Those who seek power and greed will be impoverished on this side of life, Manuana. Somehow, they have the conceptual views that their life on earth will last forever—yet this, we know, is not the case. It only takes a handful of earthly thugs to suppress weak people with the butt of a weapon. Again, those who live by the weapon will also perish the same way. Time and simple common sense always reveal this to be true. No war can bring peace to any country on your planet! As long as man assumes that he must fight in order to gain some stronghold here or there, there will be that man-created suffering. It is unfortunate, though, that so many innocent people must suffer because of some dictatorship or bad government's lust for power and wealth. Those innocent ones who do suffer, Manuana, are truly considered the humble lambs amongst the wolves. Their suffering and pain will not go without notice from God. Their state and place on this side of life will eventually compensate for it in more ways than can be humanly visualized or conceived. But, bear in mind as well, that there are many people around the world today who are suppressed or who suffer from one thing or another. These beings, too, will be compensated by God, providing their outlook and innermost feelings and sacrifices are one and in league with Him. I most humbly say to you, Manuana, and to all the world: *Pray for the conversion of sinners to God!*

I have several other questions at this time which I feel many people would like answered. Why will the medical profession not accept the value of spiritual healing and cures? Why do most scientists and many governments not accept the existence of flying saucers or even believe some people have had "visitations" from beings of other worlds? And, thirdly, the AIDS epidemic and its source—is it God's blight upon man, or is it man's blight upon man?

For your first question, Manuana, there are some in the medical profession who are keenly interested and who do believe in spiritual healing, but they are not about to come out into the open to reveal this truth. If they did, they fear they would lose their license to practice medicine, or they fear possible ridicule for their unorthodox beliefs in these matters. There are many doctors on your planet who are actually afraid to seek medical help for their own personal problems! The medical profession is like anything else on your planet, Manuana—there are some positive oriented doctors and there are some negative oriented doctors. They are not God, although there might be some who have the sick pleasure of trying to feel their importance is almighty! In any matter on your planet, it is God who actually does the healing and curing. The doctors' duties are merely to help. Faith healing is just as miraculous as a successful operation. There are teams of doctors on this side of life, Manuana, who assist both in faith healing and in normal, earthly, operative procedures. In time, there will be no operations on your planet. New methods will be shown to man by the Higher Legion of Celestials after the prophecies of old are fulfilled.

Now, your second question concerns your earthly scientists and their inability to comprehend the mere possibility that flying saucers exist. Many scientists actually do believe in their existence but would be more inclined to believe wholeheartedly if they had the pleasure of actually seeing one. Most stories or actual documentations about flying saucer sightings, personal examinations by their occupants, being taken to their planet in little more than an hour earth time, and so forth, are genuinely sincere and true! These facts should not startle anyone, simply because these Celestials are the Guardians of Light, who have been assigned to your planet from its beginnings. If you take a journey around your world, you will see countless signs and monuments that will attest to a higher intelligence that once wandered quite freely on your world. These signs and monuments were left behind by these Guardians of Light who once roamed your planet. You can go to almost any country on your planet, and you will see domes, steeples, and artifacts that actually resemble the flying saucers you see today. Your world is not the only habitable planet, Manuana; there are, without any doubts whatsoever, literally millions of habitable planets like Earth in the universes. Earth, as such, is quite isolated at the moment, but eventually man will be shown the highways and byways in outer space by these beings. Your planetary system has been mined and thoroughly explored by these beings. No time is actually lost from your world to theirs. You must also understand that these beings are still children of God, even though some of them do not look exactly like the human beings on earth. There are, nonetheless, many beings on other planets (not of your system) who look exactly like your species of life. In truth, Manuana, there are many different species of life on other planets, but they have learned to coexist with one another in God's Light. Planet Earth has yet to achieve this facet of evolution—but it must and it will!

In the beginning the gods or Celestials of Light were assigned to learn from the Light of God's Power. These beings have the power to move stars, planets, and moons at leisure— and, if necessary, they do. When you look up at the night sky, is it not amazing to see the Big Dipper and the Little Dipper? Do you think nature alone placed these constellations and figure-like star systems in their present position? It takes nature itself millions of years just to change a simple leaf. Yet man can change a leaf, a flower, or an animal to his liking through the various breeding processes which he now employs. These beings I speak of, Manuana, are so highly evolved that they are, indeed, one with God. They fly through outer space at enormous speeds, can go through so-called black holes, and can, at leisure, enter the past or future as time travellers if that is their assigned mission. Some people may consider this information as being totally unreal or illogical! No, this is not unreal or illogical. These beings have colonized other planets for millions and millions of years, and your planet is no exception to the rule. Actually, these Celestials of Light, as we call them, once replaced a smaller, hollow moon with your present larger, hollow one. This was many, many centuries ago, when great cataclysmic events took place within and around earth. There are, in fact, great secrets on the moon at present, yet to be discovered by man. He will eventually discover these truths in a peaceful way. These Celestials of Light will continue to be seen and heard from time to time until your world is ready to make its quantum leap into outer space and is prepared to accept the True Fellowship of Other Worlds. Again I say, Manuana, that the King of Light, your Messiah, will return in the flesh, and then your world will be shown the way.

Now, regarding your third question about the AIDS virus on your planet, it is regrettable, Manuana, that this blight upon man was created by man. So often, many people on your planet tend to blame God for all the wrongs that take place; yet, in reality, it is man who creates his own vices, hates, and wrongs. This virus you ask about, Manuana, is extremely destructive and deceiving; yet man, in his conquest of many things upon his planet, will search and subsequently find a cure. Be at peace, for a cure is now, at this moment, being conceived by two groups of scientists—three from the land of the Eagle and four from the land of the Lion. One cure will be in a capsule form, whereas the other will be injected through a needle. Both holistic measures will be simultaneously effective! These scientists will succeed simply because the Light of God is upon them! A breakthrough cure is foreseen and forthcoming!

I wish to ask you about life forms such as plants and animals, Oscar. Do they have their Kingdoms or Mansions on the other side of life, too? Is it wrong for man to kill and eat animals? Would man be wise by striving more towards vegetarianism?

Manuana, when a leaf falls and dies, I say to you that the soul of this leaf finds its way gently to Heaven, and there it will prosper. All plants and animals have a Kingdom on this side of life. The outer shell of earthly life may die, but the inner soul of that life lives on. Life is Eternal; Life is Truth; Life is God.

Man is conditioned to eat meat on planet Earth. As man evolves, he will eventually find various other substitutes that are better and more nourishing to his biological system. The animals on your planet instinctively know that their task on earth is to serve the higher predator, and so they do—man, of course, being the higher predator. Plants, too, know instinctively through thought vibrations that their task on earth is to serve the needs of other plants, man, animals, and, of course, insects. God's Plan of Life is infallible!

Oscar, can we talk about the power of thought? What is the best procedure on how to use thought to one's best advantage? And how does a person "dispose" of unwarranted, unwanted thoughts?

The power of thought is basically unique to each individual. Not everyone thinks the same, but through positive prayer and meditation, a person can attune his mind and soul to a oneness with self and, of course, towards the Universal Mind, the Godhead of Life.

First of all, Manuana, a prayer is both giving and asking. A person should say a prayer from the depths of his or her heart, mind, and soul with sincerity, truth, and a deep longing to become a better, wiser person. Say a prayer to God on a one-to-One basis so that you can become more intimate, more attuned to His Loving Kindnesses and Blessings. All prayer, Manuana, that is sincere, giving, asking, and loving is heard and answered in some manner; all prayer that is intended to harm or hurt another living creature will backfire on the sender sooner or later. Pray from the depths of your mind and soul. It is here where miracles actually take place! Believe what you pray for, but be sure it is of good intent.

Now, meditation, on the other hand, is a type of prayer or thinking that should be centered totally upon good thoughts towards your fellowman. No more and no less will do! Do not think about yourself in meditation! If a person decides to meditate for about three minutes a day or week, one will discover that, over a period of time, one's third eye will commence to open! And lo and behold, beautiful treasures of the soul and the so-called unknown will be revealed to him or her. There are many hidden treasures to seek and find on your earth plane, providing one is willing to open one's mind and soul to this truth.

Negative and unwarranted thoughts are common occurrences on your planet. When these occur, as you already know, Manuana, the best cure is repeating, "Sanctus, sanctus, sanctus." In translation this means, "Holy, holy, holy." Repeat "Sanctus, sanctus, sanctus" in your mind continuously until the negative or unwarranted thoughts vanish. Truly, they will! In summation, Manuana, always strive to think kindly towards all life, and truly, your life will become wiser and richer for this very simple, basic truth.

3

Death

The thought of death has mystified and troubled mankind for centuries, even up to this present time. There are many people today who honestly believe that death is a conclusion to one's life. In other words, when one dies, that is the "total" end to one's existence! Oscar, what happens immediately after the moment of death?

FIRST OF ALL, Manuana, death only occurs to the physical body of an individual, not the soul body of an individual. The physical body is born with a silver or gold cord, which is directly linked or attached to this side of life. This cord is rarely seen by the naked eye, except occasionally in astral projection. When death comes, this cord detaches itself from the earthly, physical body, and hence the soul body is now free to live on. There are many instances, however, on your earth plane when people are pronounced dead on an operating table only to be revived by your earthly doctors and nurses. In these particular cases, the silver or gold cord has not detached itself from the body, but the astral body is allowed to have a quick glimpse or two on this side of life. Hence, when people are revived in this manner, they come back with some true, marvelous stories to tell. Some see and talk to the Light in a mental way, some see their loved ones, and others see beautiful cities, and so forth. We know they must return. The Light commands them to return to earth, and they do!

At the moment of actual death, a person simply steps out of his heavy, tired or sickly physical body or physical shell only to realize that his soul body is identical to the physical body. With one's soul body a person can pinch himself, touch, shout, sing, laugh, or cry at will, if he so desires. The soul body has a finer skin than the physical body and, of course, is totally whole, pure, and healed of any earthly pain, infirmities, or sicknesses. In simple terms, if a man is without physical hands or legs on earth, he will, upon death, discover that his soul body's hands and legs are quite intact, or if a man is blind on earth, he will discover that his soul eyes can see, and so forth. Take note as well that the soul body feels much lighter than the physical body. When you walk with your soul body, it feels as though you are walking on air or walking on pillows. There is no trauma in this sense of lightness, simply because most people on this side of life enjoy this lighter-than-air feeling. The soul body can do absolutely everything the physical body does, except procreate.

Normally, Manuana, and in most so-called peaceful earthly deaths, when a person steps out of his heavy, earthly body or shell, two Angels of Light will approach that soul and ask him, "Do you wish to come to your designated Mansion now, or do you wish to remain on this earth plane for the next seven earthly days?" In most instances, the person asked generally does wish to remain on earth for that seven-day period in order to, let us say, see his own funeral, "appear" to a friend or two, visit places on earth he has never seen before, simply by thinking of the place he wishes to visit, and, perhaps, in some instances, to stay behind to say a grateful farewell to planet Earth for personal or sentimental reasons. At the end of the seven-day period, this soul is taken to its proper Mansion.

It is here that an individual will commence to thrive, learn, and prosper in glorious, wondrous ways. There are schools, universities, libraries, and halls of great learning on this side of life, Manuana, amongst millions of other wondrous sights and sounds to behold! Every soul, though, must work its way towards Heaven, as there are many Mansions to cross before Heaven is reached. Now, mind you, Manuana, there are always those special souls on earth who do reach the Greater Mansions of Light immediately upon death simply because they have learned to sacrifice their time, their space, their duties, and their life for God. There are many saints on your planet today who are totally unrecognized because of their humility, love, and servitude towards God and towards their fellowman. God seeks this humility and love and does, without a doubt, prepare a special place for those in this "special" league.

Oscar, you speak of a "peaceful death," but what about those who suddenly lose their life in a car, plane, train, or boat accident? What about those who die suddenly in a mud slide, landslide, avalanche, tornado, hurricane, earthquake, and so forth? Is there such a thing as "premature deaths" and, if so, why? Or what about those who murder others, or who decide to commit suicide?

There are, as you know, Manuana, many tragic deaths on your earth plane. Many of these souls who do pass into this world in tragic, sudden ways are immediately taken to their proper Mansion. They are actually traumatized when they see themselves in their soul bodies and simply cannot contend with the fact that they have left their world in such a sudden, tragic manner. Most people who have died in some tragedy or other had been given dreams, inner signs, and warnings that something was going to happen to them. Unfortunately, many people on your earth plane fail to heed their inner warnings, hunches, or dreams. Consequently, they shrug off these signs as being nothing to worry about. Many tragic deaths in cars, trains, planes, or boats could have been avoided if only those involved would have heeded their inner intuitive hunches and signs. Yes, Manuana, there are many premature deaths that could and can be avoided on your earth plane, providing those involved would learn to "stop, look, and listen" to their inner hunches and signs.

Now, regarding murder and suicide: first of all, taking the life of another human being is considered a very serious offence by the Laws of God. When a man murders another being on your earth plane, the soul of the murderer is not released or free to progress after death until the person he murdered actually forgives him. There is a Higher Court on this side of life—it is totally infallible! The murderer may stay in an earthly prison for many years, but, believe me, Manuana, when he enters this side of life, he immediately finds himself in another prison or in a hell state plane. God must forgive him, the person he murdered on earth must forgive him, and, as well, he must realize from the very depths of his soul the terrible act he performed upon another fellow being and upon a Child of God! The murderer on earth should ask for great forgiveness on earth now in order to find some beginning to his inner peace and solace later on. Unfortunately, far too many beings do not care, simply because they feel that spending time in prison on earth will eventually free them. No, this will not free them! There is not a crime on your planet, there is not a sin on your planet that is not seen and heard by God. God will judge these beings and their acts accordingly. There is, in truth, no escape from any evils committed against one's fellowman or against God!

Now, suicide is another foul act that is considered totally wrong by the Laws of God. When a person does commit this act, he generally finds himself in a nether plane or hell state plane! This plane consists of his own, individual, mixed-up thoughts and actions, which are revealed to him in a horrifying manner! One should never commit suicide. God gives life, and it is entirely up to Him to take life whenever He so chooses. It is not up to anyone to take life into his own hands. The consequences of these actions do not go unheard or unpunished. Yet, realize as well, Manuana, that God, the Father, is forgiving—but not until his wayward child has learned a great, vital, and perhaps long, long lesson about the value and importance of life and its true purpose.

In summation, Manuana, both murder and suicide are considered a great evil by God and should not even be remotely considered or acted upon by any of His children.

Oscar, what does an earthly individual actually take with him after death? In other words, do two people happily married on earth actually continue their marriage and their happiness on the other side? Does one's knowledge accumulated on earth or so-called prestigious "rank" on earth have a great bearing in the hereafter? What about age? If a person passes on at ninety-two years earth time, do they remain (in appearance) as ninety-two forever? What about hunger or food on the other side of life, Oscar? Also, one last question at this time—does a person take his hatreds and vices to the other side?

Manuana, two people who are happily married on earth can and do continue to work together on this side of life. Why not? Their marriage was blessed on earth and was blessed in Heaven simultaneously. Their vows were sacred and holy and so should remain that way. This type of marriage I speak of, Manuana, only belongs to "soul mate" marriages on earth. I am glad to state that there are many such marriages on your earth plane. Soul mates harmonize very peacefully in life by work-ing together and struggling together towards positive, benefi-cial goals. Actually, many soul mates begin to look alike as they grow older. Generally speaking, you might find that when one soul mate partner dies, the other partner dies shortly thereafter. They were meant to work together not only on earth but in Heaven as well! And they do! But I am also sad to report that there are many "earth mate" marriages. An earth mate marriage can end up in divorce, separation, or complete abandonment by each partner. Earth mate marriages are not happy ones—the partners tend to think and act in opposite directions of one another! There is no basic teamwork in an earth mate marriage, and generally, this type of marriage crumbles in unhappiness. There are, however, many earth mate marriages which continue to survive on your earth plane for one reason or another. But they do not survive on this side of life, Manuana. In simpler terms, soul mate partners basically think and act on a vast, horizontal plane of thought, knowl-edge, and action. In an earth mate marriage, on the other hand, one partner could be thinking calmly and wisely, whereas the other partner could be very narrow-minded and totally unrea-sonable to live with. Sometimes, both partners in an earth mate marriage have tunnel vision concepts and actions. This type of parallel thinking can and generally does bring trouble and difficulties to each partner in time to come.

Now, your next question about knowledge and rank: first of all, Manuana, the knowledge a person gleans on the earth plane should enhance the mind, heart, and soul of an individual, providing this knowledge is of good order and is wholesome. Bad knowledge or false knowledge is of no use to anyone, whether on earth or on this side of life. People take their knowledge with them to this side of life, Manuana, but must discard their superstitions, fears, hatreds, and false dogmas that they may have believed along their earthly path. Only the positive and true bits and pieces of earthly knowledge are essential to the soul here, Manuana. The soul must always strive for inner truths and perfection on this side of life in order to progress and prosper—and in order to ultimately work its way towards Heaven.

One's earthly rank does not necessarily hold much weight here, unless that earthly individual was in total league with God! There are kings and queens and many famous people on your planet who may never experience their earthly rank here. In simple terms, Manuana, "The last will come first, and the first will come last." The most humble being on your planet holds great rank here. A person who serves God and his fellowman holds great rank here. A person who saves another life holds great rank here. A person who prefers to give rather than to take holds great rank here, and so forth.

Now, concerning your third question, Manuana: when a person dies at ninety-two, upon entering his Mansion, he is given the option to revert to an age when he was most comfortable on earth. In other words, this individual at ninety-two may know that he was happiest in appearance at the age of twenty-five. Then so be it. He reverts back to this age in appearance only but still holds the knowledge or wisdom he possesses. If a child dies, on the other hand, its soul normally grows up to the age of thirty-three here, and it is at this level of appearance that this soul will continue to thrive and prosper.

As to your fourth question concerning hunger and food: no, there is no hunger on this side of life, Manuana, except in the nether regions of hell. The soul is fed by the Light of God in all areas except in the nether regions of hell. If a person demanded a steak on this side of life, Manuana, a steak would appear in front of him, but he would soon discover that this steak could not give him the sustenance required to fulfill his greater needs. There are two things the soul must have for inner food, peace, and development: the Love and Light of God.

With regards to your final question concerning hatreds and vices, Manuana: all souls must sort out and discard their hatreds and vices in order to progress on this side of life. If a person refused to discard his earthly hatreds and vices here, he could very well find himself in a lengthy or temporal hell state or have mirrored reflections of his negative actions shown to him until he is totally willing to let go of his follies and weaknesses. Each individual case is different here, Manuana, and each individual case is judged according to the folly or crime committed.

Oscar, what about the disbelievers such as the agnostic or the atheist? What is their reaction when they reach the other side? Also, what about the religious fanatics, political fanatics, or any other types of fanatics who appear to be scattered here and there on earth? How are they "assisted" on the other side?

Manuana, there are literally millions of people who disbelieved God and His marvelous wonders in some way prior to their death. Upon arriving to this side of life, they commence to see, feel, and understand the wrongs of their ways, and in most cases, these souls ask for forgiveness and, hence, are able to progress onwards. But there are always those stubborn types who refuse to admit that they are wrong. In these cases, they are given psychological and spiritual help on this side of life. Both the agnostics and atheists on planet Earth do themselves irreparable harm by trying to be so diligently different and unique in their concepts. In some cases they lose touch with the realities of life and, of course, the true Concepts of God. Their own pride and stubbornness can be the ruination of their souls! In some cases this actually happens! Their false philosophy and beliefs are corrected here but not until they learn a valuable lesson or two about the havoc they created on earth. My sincerest advice to any agnostic or atheist on your earth plane is to alter their thinking now, or, as you might say, pay the price later. And, regrettably, some do!

As to your second question about fanaticism, Manuana: it depends solely upon the degree of good or bad that is carried out by these people. If the fanatic is relatively good but does get carried away by certain beliefs, he is quick to learn and generally does rectify his problem(s) here. However, there are extreme degrees to fanaticism which require severe counselling or severe punishment here. Each case is unique, Manuana, and each case is judged accordingly. My sincerest advice to anyone partaking in fanatic temptations on your earth plane is to alter their thinking now, or, as you might say, pay the price later. Again, regrettably, some do!

The overall advice to anyone on your earth plane is simply this: if you know better, then act and live better. If you know the absolute truth about something, then speak the truth. But if you are not sure and merely speak what you feel might be true, then be mighty wary about what you tell others. Do not lead others astray by strange and foreign knowledge that bears no ground with God. There are many beliefs and doctrines on your earth plane that are antichrist concepts, created by the demons of hell. Be wary about what you say and about what you believe to be half-truths. Half-truths are not truths! Peace comes to those who are honest, sincere, and, above all, humble in their ways and actions on earth. Do not seek notoriety in anything you do, for this action alone can bring you mockery and isolation. Be true unto yourself and unto your fellowman at all times! Only the TRUTH of self and of life can come to God.

I would like very much to talk about bereavement on earth. Of what value is "sorrow" to those left behind on earth when a loved one dies? There are many people who persistently wear black or who continuously whine and pine over their earthly loss.

There is no value to sorrow nor to the ritualistic endeavors of earthlings when their loved ones depart to this side of life, to Life Everlasting. Why wear black when their loved ones here are wearing white! Prolonged mourning on earth can hold back a soul on this side of life. The mourners should learn to let go of their loved ones wisely and humbly. Their own turn will come, and sooner or later they will be together on this side of life. Feelings of self-pity often beset the mourners, but in truth, they do miss their loved ones and can only reveal their feelings through sorrow and sadness. But this, again, does not help the soul on this side of life. Very often a loved one will appear to his mourners in a dream, striving very hard to project to them that he is alive and well. Unfortunately, the mourner merely assumes that this dream is a tension dream and simply shrugs it off. What the loved one on this side of life is trying to project to his mourners is to let go of their sorrows, fears, and loneliness by carrying on with their lives in a sensible, down-to-earth fashion. Many on your earth plane simply refuse to do so. Consequently, many souls on this side of life must sleep or rest until this holdback or mourning subsides.

It is always in good order to say a prayer for loved ones on this side of life when you dream about them—always remembering to tell your loved ones to "Ask for the Light," which, no doubt, they are already presently enjoying. This spiritual code or phrase instantly assists the soul in realizing that the mourner or family member or friend on earth now understands to finally let go. And, consequently, the soul on this side of life and the family member or friend on earth left behind come to terms with the realities of carrying on with their lives.

Oscar, is there a "special prayer" from your side of life that earthlings can actually say when their loved ones do pass on? The trauma of death is very hard to bear for most earthlings unless they have a deep understanding of the hereafter, which many do not. Is there a prayer that might ease the burden of the mourner left behind on earth?

Manuana, I will give mankind this special prayer to be used wisely and comfortably when a dearly departed leaves your planet. This special prayer assigned to mankind will miraculously ease the burden of those left behind.

God of Light, God of Truth, ease my heavy-laden mind and soul. Grant me the wisdom, the insight to know better and to inwardly trust in your Kindness and Glory! Bring me to the calmness of your Heart, the insights of your Mind, and the purity of your Soul during this trying hour. Bring your legions of Angels into my soul, so that my inner strength is quickly renewed for the tasks of earth that yet lie before me. God, I am totally in Your Hands!

Saying this special prayer with love and sincerity will instantly lift the burden from the mourner. The tears will cease, and a great calmness will prevail.

Oscar, how can one actually prepare oneself for death? Many people are so frightened by the mere thought of death that they tend to ignore this eventful fact of life. Many people, as well, become so attached to earth and to their possessions that they fail to actually realize that their journey on earth is but a railroad crossing.

Live each moment, each hour, each day as though tomorrow on earth was your last. Live by the sensible Rules and Laws of God, seeded within each and every one of you. The Christ Light is within every man, woman, and child on planet Earth, but you must learn to tap this Light with Truth, Love, and Humility. Through prayer and meditation the soul grows with joys and comforts, and ultimately peace comes and grows. Enjoy your life, but live only by the truth that is within you and no other way. Do not look for lies or excuses along your earthly journey, for these deceits alone will hold you back from your rightful heritage in life. God wishes *all His children* to prosper on earth as He wishes *all His children* to prosper in Heaven. Look ahead in life with the positive "visualizations" that you will carry out some small or great task—but always remembering that death itself can come any moment, any hour, or any day of your life. Never say, "This or that could not possibly happen to me," for, in truth, it can. No soul on earth is immune to anything, so do your very best to avoid any prideful or complacent attitudes about life or about death. Always treasure the Christ Light that is within you and in front of you in life—knowing that whatever you do, or wherever you may go, God will always be by your side.

You pass through earth but once in life—treasure the privilege and honor of knowing this truth now and forevermore! And commence to believe, feel, and understand that God is always with you no matter how great or how small you may feel. And when death comes to you, be ready to open your heart, mind, and soul to the Light of God, to experience the wondrous joys of His Wisdom and His Mansions prepared just for you. You are all Children of God, so be prepared to eventually meet Him.

4

Good and Evil

Thoughts, words, and actions can be vehicles for both good and evil on earth. Why are so many people bent upon hurting their fellowman instead of helping him? Crimes of all types are being committed on this planet today like a plague, and, of course, it is the innocent victims who truly suffer. Years ago a person could leave his front doors wide open without a doubt or a worry, but, nowadays, a person has to bar his doors and windows because of widespread crime. Many people are afraid to go for an evening stroll for fear that someone might rob, attack, or even kidnap them!

SATAN IS ALIVE, well, and quite comfortable on your planet today, Manuana. If he and his hell-bound demons can get hold of any mind, heart, or soul on your planet, they truly celebrate! Far too often people give in to their sudden evil urges, assuming they will get away with their negative thoughts, words, or actions. But, sooner or later, they are found out! There is absolutely no escape from God in these matters. Any time a person commits a foul thought or deed, this action is automatically recorded within his soul. It is up to each individual on your earth plane to live a good, clean life and to try to do his very best to not be tempted by any evil thoughts, words, or actions. Swearing, for example, is one action most people partake in; yet, this foolish action does not benefit or uplift the soul! Hatred, vendettas, and pride are

other measures people employ to supposedly better themselves but sadly tend to hurt themselves instead. Many people
also find it expedient to hurt, injure, maim, or kill others
because of their own sinister and vicious attitudes and concepts
in life. But justice will prevail in these matters as well! And
then, of course, there are those infamous individuals in all
walks of life who leave a trail of sin, harm, trouble, and sorrow
along their notorious pathway to power, fame, and fortune.
Justice will prevail here, too! Some people feel, as well, that
they can get away with some perfect crime. Such unholy
nonsense! They may think they can get away with it, but in the
end, God's Laws will prevail! Evil is sin—and it is up to each
individual to account for his own personal actions and deeds in
life. A person should not blame anyone else for the wrongs he
commits. In other words, Manuana, a person cannot account
for anyone's soul in life but his own! When a soul faces the
Light of God here, Manuana, it must account for its own
actions. No excuses or manipulative guesses will do! Only the
living Truth of a soul can come to God—nothing else! So you
see, your planet is filled with all types of vices and corruptions
that only Satan gains from and revels in—and man just happens
to be his tool, his weapon which he uses and abuses in sinful,
horrifying ways! Each person on your planet is given a free
will, but each person must use this free will wisely! Unfortunately, many people give in to the whims and notions of evil
far too easily and, hence, are entrapped by the evils they create.

As I indicated before, Manuana, if a person knows better,
then, by all that is good and glorious, he should live better.
Happily, though, many people on your planet do know better
and do strive to lead happy, productive, and worthy lives, but
there are still those vast numbers of sinners and wayward
beings who simply refuse to adhere to the Christ Light within
them. And, as you already know, Manuana, it only takes an
antichrist group here and there, and an antichrist person here
and there, to make life on your planet frightfully sad, pitiful,
and questionable. But you must also realize that in this "end of
a time" now upon your planet, the Good will ultimately

surmount the Evil. Again, I beseech you and the world to *pray for the conversion of sinners to God!*

Oscar, money seems to be at the root of many evils on this planet; yet it is a common fact that money can be a positive vehicle for good if used properly and sensibly. It seems, in many ways, as though money, taxes, and greed rule this planet.

Manuana, your planet Earth has not yet evolved like the others in the Federation of Planets. The Federation of Planets I speak of does not have a money system at all! Your planet is still backward in matters concerning the true concepts of sharing, but there will come a time, "fast approaching," wherein your planet will have no need for money whatsoever! In your future Garden of Eden there will be enough food, shelter, and pleasure for every man, woman, and child. No one will go hungry, nor will greed or money exist. Man will learn to peacefully coexist hand in hand in true Brotherhood and Love. Nations will throw away their armaments and peacefully commence to toil the fields and share their common needs and common goods with others quite freely. There will be more than plenty for everyone—as only the meek will inherit your earth!

But, I reiterate, some prophecies of old must be fulfilled first before these marvelous events take place. Some people who read this message may feel this concept is absolutely ridiculous or far too unrealistic! No. It is neither. This will happen when man least expects it to happen! Today, on your planet, there is much concern about money, wealth, the stock markets, good investments or bad investments, and literally thousands of ways of utilizing get-rich-quick schemes that either succeed or fail. It is true, however, that money can be used wisely and sensibly for the time being, but it is unfortunate that many governments, money grabbing institutions, and private individuals fail to use this earthly commodity the way it should be used. If man's heart was totally pure and godly at this time, he would begin to see for himself the necessity to share freely in his temporal earthly existence. But man being the way he is and the way he feels at this time, it is highly illogical to even remotely suggest that the money situations and problems on earth will dissipate overnight. No.

When the clouds circling your planet Earth commence to move faster than the norm, when the sun appears dark red in hue, when the moon appears to spin rapidly and looks dark gray in color, when the stars in the skies appear to move, fall, and disappear, when the birds cease to sing or fly for a lengthy period of time, when phenomenal occurrences and visions are seen around the world, and, lastly, when an enormous, pure white cloud from the Lighted Gates of Heaven lands upon Holy Earth, it is then, and only then, that man will commence to know the many wrongs he has inflicted upon himself and upon his earthy planet. It is then that many miraculous events and changes will begin to occur on your planet. One of these miracles is that no money, greed, or evil will ever rule or control planet Earth again!

There are many cults, false dogmas and beliefs, and many people who proudly admit to being white and black witches and war-locks. What compels an individual to go this route in life, and what could possibly be gained from anyone even remotely hinting that they are a white or black witch or warlock?

Absolutely nothing of true value is gained by anyone admitting to being a witch or a warlock. People on your planet who do play with the so-called black arts are, in fact, playing with Satan and his legion of demons! They have no concep-tion, until they reach this side of life, of the harm and damage they have actually done to others, to themselves, and, of course, to their souls! Many of these people often say that they are very close to God and His Comforts, but, in essence, they are more close to Satan and his half-comforts and half-truths. There is no true purpose nor true need for their actions other than to seek personal notoriety and fear from others. Most of these people who do contend to be witches or warlocks are, in truth, admitting to their own folly and weaknesses. They claim to be doing good, but their so-called spells of good often project spells of evil and often backfire.

As I said before, Manuana, half-truths are not Truths! My sincerest advice to anyone following or listening to someone's false beliefs or demonic truths is to very seriously ponder their own thoughts, actions, and deeds in life. No good can come from anything that is not in tune with the Godhead of Life. There are countless cults and false dogmas on your planet that are directly linked to Satan and his legion of demons. Countless books, periodicals, tapes, and even picture shows have promoted false dogmas and beliefs. A wrong does not make a right; a false philosophy does not make a right philosophy either! People who are in league with Satan, practice his teachings. Many supposedly wise people and many famous people, too, often get on someone's false bandwagon or false teachings merely because others believe it or because the teachings appear to be so convincingly true. And when did Satan and his demons ever tell anyone the truth? Their prime aim is to lure innocent bystanders with their deceitful wiles, fancies, evil eye projections, evil thoughts, and to ultimately gain souls for the hell state planes that do exist! Listen to no false man or woman on your earth state, but, rather, walk away and follow the inner truth of love, kindness, hope, and faith that is within you. There is no easy path in life—as Satan and his legion of demons and false prophets would have everyone believe!

Oscar, will you elaborate further about Satan and his legions of demons. I, for one, do not find this particular topic as being "worthy" of discussion, but there are people on earth who should be more aware of his evil ways, habits, or appearances on earth.

Manuana, I totally concur with you, and yes, more people on your earth plane should be made aware of his beguiling ways and practices. Anyone who evokes Satan is with Satan, and this, of course, you can find in all satanic cults around your world. Witchcraft, voodoo practices, or any other form of countless black magic acts and tricks are neither wise, wholesome, nor leastwise beneficial to any soul. Anyone who practices antichrist philosophies and antichrist religions is in league with Satan. No one can serve God and Satan at the same time, as some witches and warlocks profess to do! Satan can manipulate and use anyone on your earth plane if he so chooses, but this does not necessarily mean that he will succeed. If a person is good and believes wholeheartedly in the Christ Light within him, then who on your planet could possibly harm him!

Satan and his demons simply cannot tolerate hearing this series of words being repeated: "Sanctus, sanctus, sanctus." Repeat these words continuously whenever you feel unwelcome by someone or whenever you feel you are near someone who is evil or whenever you are beset by evil thoughts or possibly tempted to do something unworthy or evil. Evil, as you know, comes in all sizes and shapes, too—so be wary of those beings who attempt to abuse, misuse, or possess you in any manner. These abusers, misusers, or possessors are following the dictates of Satan. Always follow the better dictates of your heart, mind, and soul—and Satan and his legion of demons will have to look somewhere else for their prey. Satan and his legions will not always be on planet Earth, but for the time being, always strive to do your utmost to keep your heart, mind, and soul in league with God.

What is the nature of hell? What is hell really like, Oscar? Many people on this planet feel one does not have to go too far to seek hell, simply because they feel hell is on earth already! Is there eternal damnation?

There is a vast hell state on this side of life, Manuana, which is so full of evil that it reeks of shame and sadness! This plane is quite isolated from the Godly Mansions, and it is extremely cold and dark in these satanic planes, dark caverns, and pits. The hell state planes are totally barren of any trees, plants, shrubs, flowers, or any other type of verdure so commonly enjoyed on your planet Earth. There are two conditions the soul cannot tolerate: darkness and coldness. Souls in this region are without the warmth of God's Light and suffer the pain and agony of temperatures that can quite conceivably be 180 degrees below earthly zero. There is the gnashing of teeth here, but not from any comforts, warmth, brimstone, or fire but from total, isolated darkness, coldness, and total lack of love and understanding. They continuously live each moment in their hell state not only with anguish and pain, but with all types of hellish living nightmares, sounds, and fears. The wrongs they committed on your planet are, in many ways, the wrongs they must suffer in those hell state regions assigned to them. These souls have promised allegiance to Satan for some base reason or have committed some horrendous crime against someone or against humanity for evil and base purposes and, of course, have failed immeasurably to ask for God's forgiveness. Anyone who follows Satan and his teachings, or anyone following the antichrist attitudes and concepts on your earth plane, can be assigned to these nether regions after death. This is not meant to frighten anyone on your earth plane but to advise everyone in league with evil to change their ways and habits now!

Again, I will repeat myself: *Pray for the conversion of sinners to God!* Prayers do assist some of these lost souls from time to time, not only in the hell states I speak of, Manuana, but in your world as well. There are many people on your planet today who do, in fact, create their own hell on earth for some reason or other, or who might be living under the clutches of some antichrist regime or antichrist government which ultimately makes their life on earth a living hell. When a soul is released from the clutches of Satan, there are joys reverberating throughout the Heavenly Mansions!

Now, whether or not a soul stays in eternal damnation is a question directly linked to God Himself. It is only God who can ultimately decide what soul is worthy of being released after a punishment has been served. You must, nonetheless, always remember this One Vital Universal Truth: Our Father in Heaven is Forgiving!

Is there a special prayer one can employ to avoid evil on this earth plane, Oscar, or one that may help someone who is specifically suffering from the woes of evil in some way, shape, or form?

There are literally millions of good, positive prayers written around your earthly plane that can be utilized. However, here is a special prayer for that sole purpose now, assigned to mankind to be used humbly and wisely.

God of Light, God of Truth, guide me from the clutches of evil so that I may, once more, be Your humble servant and child. I am lost and earnestly desire to be found in Your Wisdom and Light. Into Your Hands I direct my heart, mind, and soul. Into Your Hands I direct my fears. Into Your Hands I direct my unquenchable hope, faith, and trust. Father, I love You with all my being, now and forevermore!

Using this special prayer with sincerity and truth will not only uplift the troubled soul, but will instinctively give the troubled soul the spirit or drive to actually come out of its present earthly difficulties. Always remember to keep this pact with God. Far too often, people say a prayer asking for forgiveness, only to repeat the same sin or evil the next day. This will not do! This prayer must be offered sincerely from the depths of your soul—otherwise no results will ensue! All evil can be overcome through a strong self-desire to change. When a person earnestly desires a quantum change within himself, he must be willing to sacrifice old habits for new ones. It is only fear of self and fear of change that can truly hinder positive progress and results in these matters. When a change finally does take place, never look back, but go forth in the surety that you are in the Luminous Light of God.

5

Spiritual Guides

Oscar, what exactly are "spiritual guides"? Why are so many people on earth so totally oblivious to their guides or helpers "given" to them from God, and why do so many people tend to ignore the existence of spiritual guides?

MANUANA, a spiritual guide is an evolved soul on this side of life who has been assigned to help, guide, and protect another being on your planet from the time of his birth to the time of his death and even after death if the need is still there. All guides are made aware of their earthly soul assignment long before the person they are assigned to is born to your planet. Generally speaking, it normally takes one thousand years earth time for a soul on this side of life to become a Guardian Angel or what is known in some quarters as a chief guide. There are those mighty rare exceptions to the norm, however, when a soul newly arrived here actually requires a shorter training period in order to become a full-fledged guide. This rare individual would have to be highly advanced within his soul and highly attuned to God in the purest sense of the word before this could happen, but sometimes it does. Most souls on this side of life, however, must earn their way step by step before becoming full-fledged guides.

Everyone has a Guardian Angel, or what I will now refer to as a chief guide, but each chief guide has a series of fledgling guides in training who work beside him or her. For example, every male on your planet has a chief male guide with both

male and female fledgling guides working with him; every
female on your planet has a chief female guide with both
female and male fledgling guides working with her. Every
man, woman, and child on the face of your planet has a chief
guide whom, in life, they can either strive to know or ignore.
Those beings on your earth plane who are extremely psychic
or mystic certainly have a good head start in striving to see, to
hear, and to ultimately know their chief guide. This procedure, of course, may involve years of meditation and sincere
prayer before the actual gifts of prophecy, sixth sense sight,
sound, and attunement to one's guide are realized and revealed. True mediumship, or channeling, is a rare gift that
some people are born with, and, as a rule, they should always
strive to share their knowledge humbly and wisely. Some
people who are true mediums or channelers also learn this
facet of their being much later in life—through experience or
through some traumatic events that suddenly make them
aware of their inner gifts or potential. Children, for example,
are born with psychic awarenesses but tend to lose this ability
as they grow older because of their parents' views and discour-
agements, religious backgrounds, or simply because they have
been told that anything beyond the five senses should be
considered evil.

All people on your planet are psychic to some degree.
Some wish to develop their inner talents or gifts through
meditation and prayer, whereas the vast majority do not.
Those who do not wish to be bothered are normally quite
content just to abide by the inner hunches they act upon, by
the sudden awareness or inspiration that is given to them from
time to time, and by the strange coincidences that shock them
now and again. The true mediums, psychics, or mystics, on the
other hand, generally live between two worlds: their fifth
sense world and their sixth sense world. Their "field of understanding" and "inner voice" contacts are normally considered
higher and greater than the average individual's, and their
concepts about the Godhead of life are basically well-respected
on this side of life. The more attuned a person is on your side
of life, the greater his rank becomes on this side of life.

Now, Manuana, I am only speaking about those true and rare mediums, psychics, or mystics who are in league with God, His Universes, and His Children. Those who are not true mediums, psychics, or mystics, but who pretend to be, may be considered triflers or deceivers. They will have a rude awakening when they enter this side of life. There are, unfortunately, many of those triflers or deceivers on your earth plane today. They have done irreparable harm not only to themselves but to their fellowman by leading innocent people astray with their false knowledge, guesses, attunements, beliefs, and brief overshadowings by passed on souls who are not even remotely developed. My advice to anyone seeking the true knowledge and foresight of a worthy medium, psychic, or mystic is simply this: you will know them by their works. If what they tell you about yourself and your life is totally wrong, then you know you have met a trifler or deceiver. However, if what they tell you is accurate beyond any shadow of a doubt, then you know you have met a true, worthy medium, psychic, or mystic. It is really that simple. And remember, it is only the true, worthy medium, psychic, or mystic who can actually introduce you to your chief or main guide, since he is rightfully tuned in to this higher frequency of life.

Oscar, when a person passes to the other side of life, is the choice to become a guide his own choice, or is this choice made for him? Also, how can a guide know his or her earthly "protégés" before the latter's birth? Can you also explain about how many fledgling or student guides work with a chief guide?

As a soul gently evolves on this side of life, it must journey peacefully and willingly throughout all the Learning Mansions and must comprehend all the knowledge of these Learning Mansions. There are many Learning Mansions a soul must journey through before Heaven itself is reached. One's exodus towards God and Heaven is not accomplished overnight, as this could take one thousand years earth time. One thousand years earth time may be considered a long time to most people on your planet, Manuana, but no one can equate one thousand years to Eternity. When a soul arrives on this side of life, it instinctively knows that it must journey on and on until, at long last, it finally reaches God. In truth, Manuana, souls in all Learning Mansions are extremely busy and preoccupied with seeking total love, truth, and wisdom with God. To actually reach God in Heaven, a soul's Light must be in complete oneness with Him. No more and no less will do!

Now, as the soul learns and progresses in these Learning Mansions, there comes a time, after many centuries of finding God's Love, Truth, and Wisdom, that a Heavenly Ambassador is sent by God to bring a message advising this highly developed soul of its ultimate graduation to Heaven and of its future assignment to help, guide, and protect an earthly protégé yet unborn. God, the Creator of all Life, knows well ahead of time when a soul is to be born to planet Earth. So, Manuana, this, in effect, is how a Guardian Angel or chief guide is born—and how guides ultimately know ahead of time of their earthly protégés yet to come.

There are approximately twelve fledgling or student guides that work with a chief or main guide. These fledgling or student guides are not exactly ready to become full-fledged chief guides but certainly will hold this rank in due time.

My spiritual name is Manuana on the other side of life, but what is your spiritual name, Oscar? If this is given, would you prefer me to call you by your spiritual name or your earthly name?

My spiritual name is Hai-Gua, which means "spiritual waters of Truth and Light." This name was never given to you before, Manuana, for the simple reason that you have never requested this information before. Now you know!

No, Manuana, please continue to address me as Oscar Camille on your earth plane, as this earthly name is perhaps more identifiable or understandable to those you meet and greet in life. When you do reach this side of life, you will then know me as Hai-Gua. All people on your planet have a spiritual name here, but most people on your planet will never know their spiritual names until they finally arrive on this side of life.

Is a Guardian Angel or chief guide given a specific purpose for being assigned to a person here on earth? Do guides also have certain limitations?

A Guardian Angel or chief guide is, in truth, a helper or messenger from God assigned to help, guide, and advance His children on earth. And as you know, Manuana, there are many souls on your planet who can use all the help they can get. We have been assigned to assist you through the earthly protégés so assigned to us. I have been assigned to you, Manuana. So, in essence, my quest is that you assist your fellowman in the ways you have been taught and shown. With you I am pleased. There are many other protégés on your earth plane who are attempting to teach and guide mankind in similar ways, such as through teaching, music, literature, lectures, and so forth. It is regrettable, however, that many people on your earth plane fail to attune themselves to this higher knowledge or higher frequency of life so that they, too, can assist and help their fellowman. As I said to you once before, Manuana, the closer your knowledge attunement frequencies are to the Universal Concepts of All Life and God, the greater your Light, wisdom, and rank becomes here.

Far too many people on your earth plane become too preoccupied with their earthly chores and activities to even remotely think about advancing their mind, heart, and soul through meditation and prayer. Their attunement is basically earthbound and remains this way until they reach this side of life. A guide may try countless times, for example, to reach his practical or narrow-minded protégé on earth without success, simply because his earthly protégé is too busy with other mind and physical matters. Sometimes, it takes many years earth time for a guide to convince his earthly protégé to change for the better or even to reach him at all. And, sadly, sometimes a guide fails to reach his protégé simply because of his protégé's earthly difficulties and rebellious ways. But, nonetheless, a guide must stay with him whether he listens or not. Many people do not listen to that inner voice that sometimes appears to come from nowhere. Believe me, Manuana, that inner voice is, on many occasions, one's guide trying desperately to advise his earthly protégé of various warnings, positive pursuits, and right choices. But again and again this fails as many earthly protégés do not listen to, or even remotely follow, some of these inner hunches or instincts. Guides are assigned to help, guide, and advance their earthly protégés in thousands of ways—if only more people on your planet would commence to heed and take advantage of this inner truth and wisdom!

Basically, guides have no limitations, as they are given free rein by God to carry out His Work. A possible limitation that most guides might experience while on earth is not being assigned the right to actually appear face to face with an earthly protégé. There are those mighty rare exceptions, of course. You have been privileged to see my head, hands, feet, and, of course, a part of my robe, Manuana. You have also been privileged to see several other Great Master Angels whom I humbly love and respect. In almost all instances on your planet, people cannot see us because they are not attuned to this higher, Heavenly frequency of life. Unless that attunement is reached, a person on your planet cannot possibly see us unless so assigned by God Himself. The many other souls you have seen from this side of life, both in the past and even now, Manuana, have not yet reached this higher frequency I speak about.

Why are psychics not able to help themselves as frequently as they do others? Many psychics, for example, are not always given the forewarning of a death, sickness, or accident within their own family core—yet they can forecast these events with astounding accuracy when someone else is involved.

The vast majority of true psychics very rarely ask for themselves. They would rather concentrate on the pressing needs of others. You must remember that the gift of sixth sense sight or prophecy is one that is meant to be shared with others and not confined to self. All true psychics understand this concept within their assigned work. The vast majority of true psychics struggle from day to day like anyone else, asking nothing for themselves but always remembering the need to serve their fellowman. If a death, a sickness, or an accident occurs within their family, they may sometimes sense that something is wrong, but they do not always pinpoint their depressed feelings as indicating a death, a sickness, or an accident within their own family. Many people on your planet who are not psychic feel that all true psychics should continuously be tuned in to all problems and to everyone around them both day and night. No, this is not so, nor can this be.

There are, nonetheless, many true psychics on your earth plane who are made aware when something is amiss within their family circle, and, of course, it is up to them to either forewarn the family circle or abide by the inevitable consequences. For example, if a psychic was made aware that his or her elderly grandfather was about to die, then it would be up to that psychic to either reveal this news to the family circle or to be still and quiet. A timely death is a fact of life that must be faced by everyone on your earth plane. And, too, untimely deaths, sicknesses, or accidents are not always foreseen by true psychics nor can they be. Basically, Manuana, most forewarnings true psychics receive are handled both calmly and wisely. Most true psychics go from day to day carrying out their earthly and psychic duties as best they can. Strive to remember, as well, that no one is absolutely all-knowing or all-wise on your earth plane, nor should anyone expect this of a true psychic.

Oscar, sometimes psychics are very vague when they try to pinpoint the location of a crime or of some period of time when something, good or bad, is to occur. Can you explain?

Some true psychics on your earth plane are very gifted in these areas, whereas some true psychics are gifted in other areas of perception, prophecy, and help. Not all true psychics are gifted in the same way. Many, of course, are more talented and proficient in some areas than others. The one thought to remember here, Manuana, is that all true psychics do sincerely strive to assist their fellowman in some manner. Along their progress in life, they may have their so-called perceptive hits and misses, but as a whole, their perceptive hits far outweigh their perceptive misses.

Yet, many people on your earth plane might ask, "If these true psychics are of God, why do they have any perceptive failures at all?" That answer is quite simple. They are not infallible, nor were they ever programmed to be all-knowing or all-wise on your earth plane. No one on your earth plane is! Who on your earth plane can honestly say that he has never made a mistake or two? No one! Everyone on your planet makes mistakes, but as long as they learn to grow and prosper from their mistakes, then all is well. Far too often, people on your earth plane tend to "cast stones" on various groups of people, whether they are true psychics or not, without actually realizing that they are, in fact, casting a stone or two upon themselves. Always love and serve your fellowman in some small or great way, as this act alone will bring you closer to God! Leave God's Judgments to God! Many true psychics on your earth plane today are following this conceptual truth, Manuana.

How can a person actually contact his spiritual guide? Is there a simple method or two a person could employ, Oscar?

The best known method to contact one's chief guide is through a true medium, psychic, or mystic. These true mediums, psychics, or mystics are extremely rare. They have been born this way and are in league with this higher frequency in life. Do not expect these individuals to flaunt their gifts or advertise in any newspapers. They do not. Their outstanding work speaks for itself, and essentially, the only way to meet them is by word of mouth—if one is so fortunate. However, if a person is psychically inclined, he may try to contact his own chief guide through calm meditation and earnest prayer. The meditation I speak of is quite simple but must be practiced no more than three minutes a day or no more than three minutes a week. In this meditation, think kindly about your fellow-man; think about the poor people on your earth plane having shelter and food in their mouths; think kindly about the sickly and infirm in hospitals around your world getting better; think kindly and hope earnestly for peace on earth, and so forth. Think about anything positive and good, but *do not* think about yourself while you meditate, and *do not* meditate beyond the three-minute assigned time. In this simple meditation, positive thoughts are sent out into the Cosmos and will be returned to planet Earth with positive results, both here and there. The sitter or meditator may never know the good he or she has done, but so be it; it is much better that way. By faithfully following this meditative procedure, a person will grow and prosper both inwardly and outwardly. Eventually, a beautiful package from the Cosmos will be returned directly to the deserving sitter or meditator. The third eye will commence to open, and beautiful treasures from the soul will commence to come forth. But remember this: when this happens, be prepared to dedicate your talents or your gifts to your fellow-man. If you knock on that door and that door opens, you are now responsible and obligated to fulfill your new found perceptions in life. *Do not flaunt your talents or gifts; use them wisely; otherwise you will stumble, fall, and fail!*

This method, of course, can take many, many years. Do not expect overnight results, for this will not happen. A person psychically inclined wanting this personal contact must be extremely deserving, dedicated, sincere, and loyal to all of God's Truths before any contact can be made. Without any form of dedication to one's fellowman, or loyalty towards God, a person should not even bother to try. They will be defeated even before they begin. Only the purest of heart, mind, and soul need try, and even then, the purest minded individuals must constantly and diligently strive to be better and wiser in their daily thoughts and deeds. Very few, except for those rare individuals born with this gift on your earth plane, can or will meet this criteria, Manuana.

6

Spiritual Mansions

Oscar, how many Heavenly Mansions are there on the other side of life? Also, can you describe them?

THERE ARE SIX DISTINCT Learning Mansions before Heaven, which is the seventh Mansion, can be reached. Each Learning Mansion is composed of countless inner Mansions where a soul commences to live, learn, and eventually prosper. Heaven itself cannot be reached overnight—a soul must earn its way to this Glorious State of God through patience, time, and effort. I will now describe these Heavenly States, Manuana.

Most people on your planet will eventually find themselves on the first Learning Mansion upon their passing to this side of life. The souls I speak about here, Manuana, are those who have sinned to some degree along their journey in life. The first Learning Mansion, on a vast scale, is very similar in appearance to planet Earth, except the colors, sounds of music, and sights of all life here are more pronounced and far more beautiful to behold. The inner Mansions, too, bear resemblance to your planet in their own, different, unique manner of beauty and appearance. Some of these inner Mansions are small, and some are enormous, appearing like a world within a larger world or a vast series of small wheels within a larger wheel, so to speak. It is within these inner Mansions that souls must commence to finally learn the wrongs of their ways. Many people on your planet who continuously sin in some manner, but whose sins do not warrant hell, will eventually find themselves here. There is an inner Mansion available for every person on your planet, depending on the basic sins they have committed while on earth. There can be many or few souls within each distinct inner Mansion, but this, of course, depends solely upon the minor or greater sins they once committed.

All souls within these inner Mansions are guided by Higher Angelic Beings assigned by God, and, in some rare cases, they are guided by their own Guardian Angel or chief guide. All inner Mansions are composed of schools, houses, tall buildings, small buildings, farms, hospitals, churches, roads, highways and byways, forests, flowers, grass, mountains, rivers, lakes, and just about every conceivable known object and convenience you have on planet Earth. The soul will eventually let go of these outward similarities and conveniences only to retain the inward beauty and peace of God's Wisdom that they must gather along their way. The Animal Kingdom can, as well, cross over into the first Learning Mansion which, in effect, would allow an individual soul the opportunity to reclaim their long lost pet for a brief period of time. The pet, however, must return to its Animal Kingdom where it, too, must grow and prosper. Eventually, both souls will meet again, but not until Heaven is reached.

There are many areas of learning and growing within these inner Mansions, which, in many cases, may involve spiritual self-development through reading, Angelic Lectures, or some form of mirrored reflections of self or psychological help and assistance through reading, Angelic Lectures, or some form of mirrored reflections of self. There is no need for food here, nor is there any form of procreative activities here, as the soul body is fed by the Light of God.

Anyone, whether rich, famous, or poor, who is prideful, greedy, vain, boastful, possessive, spiteful, deceptive, indifferent, faultfinding, gossipy, jealous, has failed to show gratitude towards God and his fellowman, has continuously used God's Name in vain for selfish or personal reasons, has failed to transform his earthly hate into love and forgiveness, has used his earthly knowledge, wisdom, talents, or gifts without virtue, hope, and love, or used his talents or gifts for some other false, selfish, personal reasons and gain, has failed to become intimate with God and His Teachings through his daily activities and practices, or has failed in some way to conduct himself properly and productively on your earth plane will ultimately find himself on this first Learning Mansion. This first Learning Mansion is by no means a hell state but should be considered more of a cleansing or therapeutic state where souls come to be purged of all their sins. The hell states I spoke about previously, Manuana, are quite remote from this first Learning Mansion, and, of course, souls assigned to a hell state have committed some greater, more profound, horrendous sins towards God, towards His Universal Teachings, and towards His Children. All crimes committed against God are judged accordingly by the Light of God, and a person on your earth plane would have to be extremely sinful to be assigned to a hell state region. There are, as well, some Higher Courts between the first Learning Mansion and the hell state regions where some souls are tried for their crimes against God and His Children. Some of these souls will never enter the first Learning Mansion, but will be assigned into hell. *All souls who pass through the light of the first Learning Mansion will eventually reach Heaven!*

Now, when a greedy, wealthy man passes to this side of life, he will be assigned to an inner Mansion or two wherein he must commence to learn the wrongs of his ways. If, for example, while in the learning stages, he literally demands to have all his earthly wealth and all his earthly property brought to him, he will then be given that right to actually see and to actually have this so-called wealth and property he supposedly left behind on earth. His wealth and his property will appear in front of him, but sooner or later he will come to the realization that not one thought of his earthly, materialistic wealth and property can bring him closer to God. When he finally comes to this understanding, the wealth and property he demanded to see and to have will disappear in front of him. Hence, he will have learned a valuable lesson: to finally let go of all his materialistic greed, wants, and needs. He finally comes to the realization that he must move forward in order to reach Heaven—and he does! He must continue to learn in this inner Mansion for similar false thoughts or actions, or he is taken to another inner Mansion in order to free and purge his soul from some other sin he once committed. All sins of the soul must be cleansed in this first Learning Mansion—no matter how stubborn souls wish to be or how long they wish to take. Some souls can be very wayward and stubborn here if they so choose, but sooner or later, they will discover that they must let go of old ways and commence to adopt new ways in order to progress and prosper.

Another example is when a famous, prideful individual enters this first Learning Mansion. This prideful individual often looked down upon the poor and needy on earth, was prejudiced, and could not be bothered to help or assist anyone but himself. In his inner Mansion, he will be serving the needy and the poor until he finally learns humility and comes to the realization of all the wrongful prejudices and feelings he once committed on your earth plane. So the truth that the first will come last, and the last will come first holds some validity here! However, those whom he is serving, who feel their needs and wants were not fulfilled on earth and who wish to make up for lost time, will also come to the realization that to be constantly served, pampered, and spoiled are negative means leading towards self-love, which cannot in any way bring them closer to God. Hence, those poor and needy souls being served will eventually come out of their negative, lethargic ways, wants, and needs, too.

There are literally millions of lessons to be learned in this first Learning Mansion, and just as many methods are employed to ultimately show and teach the soul its way to finally let go of old habits and sins. Souls eventually elevate, help one another, discover new concepts about themselves, life, and God, and, at long last, come to terms with themselves through peaceful, truthful, loving actions, thoughts, and insights. They finally commence to gain greater wisdom about God's Truth, Love, and Compassion. All souls who enter the Light of the first Learning Mansion must eventually free themselves of all their sins before they can possibly enter the next higher plateau known as the second Learning Mansion. In some cases, it may take a soul a year or two, a decade or two, or even a century or two, to finally elevate from this first Learning Mansion to the second Learning Mansion. This time element rests solely with the soul and its total commitment and willingness to learn and to be free of all sin. Most people in this first Learning Mansion are more than busy and anxious to repair their ways and their sins, and desire earnestly to move on to the next Learning Mansion as quickly as possible.

And there comes a time when God's Light welcomes them into the second Mansion of Learning, with their finest garments, with their elevated, sinless thoughts, and with their recently acquired purified soul Light.

There is no joy on your earth plane that could even remotely describe the awe, peace, and beauty the soul experiences within the second Learning Mansion. Only a child on your earth plane, who is angelic in every sense of the word, could possibly sense this inner peace for a brief moment or two at birth. In essence, souls on the second Learning Mansion are, indeed, pure, innocent, and, in more simplistic terms, like a newborn child. There is a multitude of inner Mansions here, too, which must be explored, and ultimately learned, along the soul's lengthy journey. Normally, a soul's journey in this pure and holy second Mansion takes a century or two earth time before it can progress to the third Learning Mansion. The buildings within this second Learning Mansion are both high and low, are perfectly white in color, and have an aura about them of totally rejoicing in God's Love and Compassion. The mountainous valleys, plains, trees, flowers, rivers, lakes, streams, and fountains are crystal clear to look at and appear to sparkle with infinite love and sing with infinite praises to every soul within this second Learning Mansion. Each inner Mansion, again, is like a series of smaller worlds within a larger world or a series of smaller wheels within a larger wheel, except that now everyone and everything both within and around these inner Mansions are boundlessly more beautiful, more peaceful, and more loving to behold. There are higher learning schools, universities, and, of course, libraries within the inner Mansions where a soul commences to learn and prosper. There is a host of Great Angelic beings, Cosmic Masters, and, on occasion, one's Guardian Angel, who assist souls along their wondrous, newfound joys and experiences here. There are many inner Mansions, for example, that not only seem to have the appearance of galaxies, but which are, in truth, actual galaxies not seen by earth.

You see, Manuana, it is upon entering this second Learning Mansion that a soul finally dons its wings. Now, these are not the bird wings you often see on angelical beings in religious pictures or paintings on your earth plane. No. The soul can now travel quickly to some of these distant galaxies or star systems by pure thought and by pure will. Instantly, a soul can travel to certain star systems in order to explore and to learn more about God's Genesis and Wonders! This newfound way to travel is so exciting and exhilarating to most souls here that many would prefer to constantly fly instead of walking when the need arises. But, nonetheless, walking is still a joyous pastime which all souls continue to partake in and respect.

Let it be known, as well, that upon entering this second Learning Mansion, the "mind" of the soul now becomes totally open and functional to its true genius potential. You must understand, Manuana, that the earth mind is very limited and barely open to its full potential. The sinless soul mind in this second Learning Mansion is now equivalent to a combined host of geniuses on your earth plane. The soul mind of an individual will continue to reach out, learn, and prosper as it gently earns its way towards Heaven. There are many libraries within some of the inner Mansions, and it is the duty and practice of each soul to read the countless books contained within these libraries. The books themselves look like books you have on earth, except each book with a given title contains blank pages. Each soul picks up a book, opens it up, and—lo and behold!—the blank pages now become written with Wisdom, Philosophy, and Literature from the Mighty Pen of God, His Angels, His Higher Legion of Celestials, and, in some cases, from some special authors who once lived on your earth plane and were inspired by God to write, and from some present-day authors on your earth plane who continue to be inspired by God. You will find no books of fiction, no books of violence, nor will you find any books of false knowledge, false teachings, or false inspirations anywhere within all the Heavenly Mansions. Many writers and philosophers, upon passing to the first Learning Mansion, have had great regrets and sorrow for not having written something more worthy of their genius and talents. You see, Manuana, all worthy books on your planet are automatically published here too, but they must be of the purest Light and must be totally in league with God's Teachings and Laws.

The same applies to music, which must be both inspiring and in league with God's Teachings and Laws. The music within the inner Mansions is totally awe-inspiring, fulfilling, and joyous beyond anything imaginable on your earth plane. If you were to listen to an inspired song on your earth plane and were to augment the beauty of that song one hundred times hundred, then you might have a brief idea of what I speak about, Manuana. Again, there have been many singers and composers who, upon passing to the first Learning Mansion, have had great regrets and sorrow for not having sung or written something more worthy of their gifts and talents while on earth. There are some earthly pieces of music here as well but only from those beings who were or are deserving and who have been inspired by God. The vast majority of so-called bestselling books and songs on your earth plane will continue to remain on earth simply because they are in keeping with the mentality of your earth's many practical wants and needs.

But to continue, the soul in the library now reads the book and continues to read others here and there until eventually all the books have been read and absorbed within the libraries of one inner Mansion. This does take time—as certainly these books cannot all be read overnight, and, of course, they are not. Eventually, the soul is ushered into more libraries within other inner Mansions where more books must be read and absorbed. Souls also attend various schools and universities of purer thought where Angelic Lectures of a High Order, Questions of a High Order, and ultimately Answers of a High Order take place. No soul within these inner Mansions can leave a library, school, or university without being totally fulfilled and contented by what has been read, taught, or learned. It is the souls' Heavenly Duty and Obligation to totally comprehend both the difficult and sometimes simple ways in which God performs His Wondrous Universal Miracles, Gifts, Healings, and a host of other positive Actions of Life. And all souls do so more than willingly! This second Learning Mansion, with its multitude of inner Mansions, is, in many respects, like an enormous oasis of true inner Peace, inner Joy, and inner Learning.

Eventually, when the souls have learned and absorbed all those vast secrets and vast treasures within this second Learning Mansion, they, once more, don their finest raiments, pure thoughts, and knowledge and are ushered into the third Learning Mansion with yet a purer, brighter soul Light. Angelical choir voices and trumpets can be heard at a distance during this ceremonious occasion, as songs of Heavenly Praise and Heavenly Welcome usher in all the souls who have now graduated into their third Learning Mansion. The third Learning Mansion literally swells with great peace, joy, and awe-inspiring Philosophy from the Mighty Pen of God. Here a soul will meet, mingle with, and ultimately learn from a multitude of Celestial Beings of Light from distant star systems as well as from other Angelical Beings, Cosmic Masters, and from one's Guardian Angel, if so directed. There are many buildings here, which are both high and low, pure white in color, and tend to display an aura of golden light both within and around them. There is a multitude of inner Mansions within the third Learning Mansion, and, again, these inner Mansions are like seeing a series of smaller worlds within a larger world or a series of smaller wheels within a much larger wheel. Each inner Mansion within the third Learning Mansion now appears to be much greater in size than those of the second Learning Mansion. Everything you see, feel, or experience within the third learning Mansion and its multitude of inner

Mansions is even more clear and more breathtaking than what the soul experienced in the second Learning Mansion. In fact, Manuana, each Learning Mansion is like taking a quantum step closer to God's Infinite Light, Love, Knowledge, and Wisdom. The schools, universities, and libraries here are of yet a Higher Order, because it is, once more, the souls' Heavenly Duty and Obligation to totally comprehend the Philosophic Parables, Wisdom, and Teachings assigned by God and His Teachers. Within the multitude of inner Mansions, there are several other distant galaxies now open for each soul to explore and comprehend. There is also one vast universe within this third Learning Mansion, which will be assigned to each soul to ultimately explore and comprehend as well.

Needless to say, Manuana, most souls present here become ecstatic with this news! Their soul mind and soul body travel, a treasured Gift from God, still continues to hold a great fascination for them! The several galaxies and one universe I speak of, Manuana, are unseen on your earth plane. You must realize that God's Heavens literally abound with higher forms of life hitherto unknown to planet Earth. When a soul does venture forth to its assigned galaxy or vast universe I speak of, Manuana, it instantly travels there by pure thought and by pure will. Once there, the soul travels from planet to planet within the assigned galaxy or universe and commences to see, hear, and comprehend the many wonders and marvels of God's Children who live, abide, and flourish on these distant planetary systems. There are countless star systems where knowledgeable beings are mentally, physically, and spiritually light-years ahead of earth's knowledge and understanding. There is a multitude of planets with beings who look exactly like earth people; yet, there are just as many habitable planets with beings who are somewhat different in appearance. Some of these different beings are small or tall, lean, ash in color, have big eyes, and small nose and mouth, whereas some are extremely tall beings with high foreheads, large eyes, small nose and mouth, and can either be ash in color or white in color. There are some smaller planets which harbor beings no bigger than three to ten inches tall who, in many respects, look like earth beings except for their size. There are some larger planets which harbor beings as big as giants, and these, too, look like earth beings except for their weight and height. There are some beings on some star systems with white hair, brown skin, high foreheads, two, large, piercing eyes, and small nose and mouth, who talk to one another mentally and who walk upon their planets suspended on air. There are some tall beings, who have white, brown, or yellow skin, white hair, kindly eyes, a variety of nose shapes, and kindly mouths, who can, at will, disappear in front of your eyes and reappear whenever they so choose. These latter beings are very highly evolved and can, in many respects, be called the Masters of their Universe.

And, of course, Manuana, there are millions of other types of beings in the Cosmos unfamiliar to earth and its people. Even so, and in spite of their so-called differences, they are and will continue to be God's Loving Celestial Children. Of all the species of insects you have on your earth plane, Manuana, you could multiply each individual species times ten hundred billion to give you some inkling as to approximately how many planets actually harbor life in the infinite Cosmos. The soul's great journey within the third Learning Mansion will take a century or two earth time, but you must be aware, Manuana, that, as each soul evolves inwardly and explores outwardly, there is an infinite happiness, an unquenchable desire to constantly want to know even more than what has hitherto been experienced. The soul mind is like a "thirsty sponge" whose total quest towards God yearns to be fulfilled and consummated in His Light, His Love, and His Wisdom. As the soul mind and soul body progress here, they adapt to its brighter Light of inner peace, harmony, and wisdom! The Heavenly Music within all the inner Mansions swells with such joy and pleasure, Manuana, that no soul can cease to smile or to express its infinite happiness for just being a part of God's Great Cosmic Plan.

When the assigned portion or fraction of God's Laws within Laws, God's Knowledge within Knowledge, and God's

Wisdom within Wisdom is learned, digested, and experienced within this third Learning Mansion, the soul is then cloaked with a purer, brighter soul Light. It is at this time that the soul is ushered towards a golden gate which leads into the valley of the next Learning Mansion. Angelical choirs and Heavenly Music with trumpets can be heard loud and clear as the soul gently walks forth with its newest raiments, purer thoughts, and greater knowledge into the fourth Learning Mansion.

The fourth Learning Mansion, with its multitude of inner mansions, is vast in size, and even though each soul present here has learned to contain its curiosity somewhat, it cannot help becoming totally immersed in the awesome beauty, joys, and realities. The souls once more meet, mingle with, and ultimately learn from newly assigned Highly Evolved Angelic Beings, Cosmic Masters, one's Guardian Angel, if so assigned, and, lastly, from many other Celestial Beings of Light who originate in distant universes unknown to earth. The many high and low buildings within the inner Mansions are of a purer white color than previously seen and tend to radiate a type of golden-blue aura both within and around them. To merely touch the walls of one of these buildings, a soul simply knows that they were all "created" by the Hand of God Himself. The mountainous valleys, plains, rivers, and lakes within some of the inner Mansions are so peacefully bright and joyous to behold that each soul literally feels the praises of life emanating from every living source present. A flower alone is so colorful, sweet smelling, and gripping to see that each soul present can actually feel and understand its life's attunement and service to God. These inner Mansions are like seeing a series of greater worlds within a larger world or a series of larger wheels within a much greater wheel. The music within all the inner Mansions is more acutely defined and appears to be more intimate with each soul present. Each note, each sound of music heard appears to be written for each personal soul present! It is also a great experience to see the multitude of souls arrayed in their finest, colorful raiments. These raiments are like silk, yet can be described as being one thousand times purer than your finest silk on earth. No soul is ever blinded by another's Light or aura here, but I will say that a physical earth being on your planet would be. All the schools, universities, and libraries are yet of a Higher Order, as it is, once more, the soul's Heavenly Duty and Obligation to totally comprehend the Wisdom and Teachings assigned by God and His Teachers. Within the multitude of inner Mansions, there are five newly assigned galaxies to explore, along with two newly assigned universes to explore and ultimately comprehend. And, of course, this will eventually be consummated, as the mind soul constantly longs to know more and more. The schools and universities of Greater Thoughts and Wisdom are kept busy, as well as the multitude of libraries where rows and rows of Heavenly Books must be read and understood. And, of course, they eventually will be read and digested. Some books within some of the libraries are rather unique. A soul opens the first page to one of these books and actually sees the entirety of this book's wisdom and knowledge in a type of picture-show fashion. You must understand, Manuana, that as God's Wisdom is being taught and learned on this fourth Learning Mansion, you could almost say at this time that the souls present here have evolved one light-year ahead of earth's thinking and knowledge. In order to reach Heaven, each soul must strive diligently to become as one with God, knowing, as well, that its knowledge, wisdom, and Light must be totally in tune with His Knowledge, Wisdom, and Light.

You must remember, as well, that God's Wonders are Infinite and that each inner Mansion within all the Learning Mansions brings the soul closer and closer to the purest realities of His Teachings and Laws. God desires no flaws in His Children but desires only the purity of His Children's Light and Wisdom. This does take time; however, the soul's ultimate quest to be with God will eventually be reached. Normally, the time spent within this fourth Learning Mansion takes two centuries earth years, but there are always those very special souls who seem to evolve more quickly than others. And some souls can accomplish this feat within an earth's century.

When the assigned portion or fraction of God's Laws within Laws, God's Knowledge within Knowledge, and God's Wisdom within Wisdom is learned, digested, and experienced within this fourth Learning Mansion, the soul is then cloaked with yet a purer, brighter soul Light. The soul is gently ushered towards yet another golden gate which leads into the Higher Realms of the next Learning Mansion. And, once more, Angelical choirs can be heard singing their praises to God with loving joy and peace as Heavenly Music swells with awesome splendor! The soul gently walks forth with its newest raiments, purer thoughts, and greater knowledge into the valley of the fifth Learning Mansion.

The fifth Learning Mansion, along with its multitude of inner Mansions, is also very vast and, needless to say, very beautiful to behold! Each Learning Mansion is always more refined and always more glorious and intricately more pure than the previous one. It is here where a soul will meet, mingle with, and commence to learn from a host of newly assigned Angelical Beings, Cosmic Masters, one's Guardian Angel, if so directed, and, again, from a different selected host of Celestial Beings of Light who emanate from different universes not seen by planet Earth. The buildings within the inner Mansions are high and low, are pure white in color, and tend to radiate an aura of gold-blue-purple, both within and around them. These buildings I speak of, Manuana, are now much larger in size and in many respects appear to be a conglomerate of smaller cities within larger cities. Each building appears to convey a great personal warmth and love towards each soul present. Of course, there are vast mountainous valleys, plains, rivers, and lakes within many of the inner Mansions as before. Each inner Mansion is so intense in its assigned radiated Light and Beauty that all souls present can profoundly feel their closeness to God and Heaven. To describe the feeling here, Manuana, a person on your earth plane would have to recall one of the greatest moments of happiness ever experienced on earth and then augment that happiness by one million times. This thought alone should give you some idea as to how each soul constantly feels within the fifth Learning Mansion. Once again, Manuana, these inner Mansions are like seeing a series of greater worlds within a larger world or a series of larger wheels within a much greater wheel.

Everything a soul sees, hears, or touches within the inner Mansions has an aura of God's Great Love and Wisdom about it. All the schools, universities, and libraries are of a still Higher order, as it is, once more, the soul's Heavenly Duty and Obligation to totally comprehend the Wisdom and Teachings assigned by God and His Teachers. Within the vast multitude of inner Mansions, there are now seven newly assigned distant galaxies to explore, along with five newly assigned distant universes to explore and ultimately comprehend. The necessity to learn more about God's Highly Evolved Children in the vast galaxies and universes is, of course, an absolute must! Naturally, this task will ultimately be done, as each soul mind more than willingly accepts its highly advanced, quantum missions with great ease and pleasure. The elevated concepts of Greater Thoughts and Wisdom are constantly being taught at all the schools and universities as well. The libraries, too, hold vast amounts of Heavenly Books, which must be read and ultimately understood. This learning process may, at times, sound mundane to some earth beings, but, believe me, Manuana, there is such joy in learning all about God's Knowledge and Holy Mysteries that the souls present here simply overflow with happiness to be given this glorious opportunity! The music within all the inner Mansions and books within all the libraries literally swell with an ultimate Holy Joy; yet, truthfully, this Holy Joy is conveyed to each and every soul in a personal, intimate way. Each soul gleans something extremely profound and extremely joyous from the music it hears and from the host of books it reads. In fact, Manuana, each soul present is being intimately tuned to the Music of God and to the Mighty Words of God! At this point in time, Manuana, you could almost say that each soul present here has now evolved two light-years ahead of earth's thinking and knowledge. The time spent within this fifth Learning Mansion is approximately two centuries earth years.

When the assigned portion or fraction of God's Laws within Laws, God's Knowledge within Knowledge, and God's

Wisdom within Wisdom is learned, digested, and experienced within this fifth Learning Mansion, the soul is then cloaked with yet a purer, brighter soul Light. The soul is then gently ushered towards another golden gate which leads into the much Higher Realms of the next Learning Mansion. As the soul gently walks forth with its newest raiments, purer thoughts, and greater knowledge into the valley of the sixth Learning Mansion, one can hear Angelical choirs and Heavenly Music with breathtaking peace, splendor, and awe!

The sixth Learning Mansion, along with its multitude of inner Mansions, is extremely vast and, of course, even more glorious and more beautiful to behold! It is here where a soul will meet, mingle with, and commence to learn from a host of yet other assigned Angelical Beings, Cosmic Masters, one's Guardian Angel, if so directed, and, again, from a wide selection of Celestial Beings of Light who originate from different universes not known to planet Earth. It is also here where souls will commence to see a host of ancient Heavenly Ambassadors. These Heavenly Ambassadors abide in Heaven and can be considered God's Royal Emissaries. It is their task, at this time, to assign the vast majority of souls within the sixth Learning Mansion to their yet unborn protégés on earth, as well as to their yet unborn protégés on other, more advanced star systems.

You must also be aware that all highly evolved beings on other star systems pass on to this side of life just as they do on earth, except that their physical life span is much longer than that of earth people. Some beings on other planets may live up to two thousand to ten thousand years earth time in their physical body and mind, whereas some may live much longer in their physical body and mind. Some of these highly evolved beings, such as the Masters of the Universe, for example, go directly to Heaven upon passing away on their planets, whereas some other highly evolved beings on other star systems may go directly into the fifth or sixth Learning Mansion before Heaven is reached. All souls who enter directly into the fifth or sixth Learning Mansion upon passing away must, however, comply with all the Laws of Evolvement in order to enter Heaven. These highly evolved beings, or Celestials of

Light, never have to go into the first, second, third, or fourth Learning Mansion after death simply because their knowledge has already excelled beyond that level of Thought.

The Celestials of Light, working with a soul in the third, fourth, fifth, and sixth Learning Mansions, have already reached Heaven and have been specifically assigned to work in these particular Learning Mansions. There are some instances on your earth plane whereby some earth people have been assigned a Guardian Angel not from your world at all but from some distant star system. Or, by the same token, a special soul from planet Earth now in the sixth Learning Mansion may be assigned to an unborn soul yet to be born on a planet of another universe. Most souls in the sixth Learning Mansion, nonetheless, will eventually become Guardian Angels after Heaven is reached, as their graduated assignment has to be known long before a soul is born to a planet. There are some select souls here, as well, who will be assigned other Heavenly Missions and Tasks due to their unique talents and gifts granted by God Himself.

It is, without any doubt, an honored privilege for any soul within the sixth Learning Mansion to actually see these Royal Emissaries, to talk to them, and to be with them for even a moment or two! They tend to radiate a majestic and exalted Light, Warmth, Truth, and Love about them and tend to be very decisive and quick in all their actions. They are dressed in the purest raiments from Heaven and instinctively know each individual soul's entire history. When these Royal Emissaries have completed their tasks here, they once more return to Heaven. Needless to say, Manuana, after this Royal Visitation, each soul present here is glorified by the beautiful sounds of music created by God Himself! Each soul bows in humility, thankfulness, and prayer for its future graduated task.

The buildings within the inner Mansions are extremely high in some areas and relatively low in others, are pure white in color, and tend to radiate an aura of yet a purer white color both within and around them. This white aura both within and around these buildings is exhilarating to behold and tends to express the individual purity of each soul present within the sixth Learning Mansion. The walls within and around these buildings appear to actually sing praises to God! In many respects, these massive to low buildings now appear to be a conglomerate of large cities within greater-sized cities. In many of the inner Mansions, one can also see a host of beautiful mountainous valleys, plains, rivers, and lakes which appear to be even more distinct and more purified than ever before, as, indeed, they are! Each inner Mansion glows with the Comfort and Light of God and is individually felt by each soul present, who now knows Heaven itself is but a breath away from being a true reality! These inner Mansions, once more, Manuana, are like seeing a series of greater worlds within a larger world or a series of larger wheels within a much greater wheel. All the schools, universities, and libraries are of a still Higher order, as it is, once more, the soul's Heavenly Duty and Obligation to totally comprehend the Wisdom and Teachings assigned by God and His Teachers. Within the vast multitude of inner Mansions, there are, again, seven newly assigned distant galaxies to explore, along with five newly assigned distant universes to explore and ultimately comprehend. All this learning and all this exploration, of course, will eventually be done, with great anticipation, with great zeal, and, lastly, with great accomplishment and success! In many respects, this sixth Learning Mansion is like seeing a young eagle fly on earth, with all its ingrained knowledge and wisdom! So, too, the soul here has now gleaned experience and wisdom that could be considered three light-years ahead of earth's thinking and knowledge. The time spent within this sixth Learning Mansion is approximately two centuries earth years but remember, as well, that as each soul progresses and accomplishes its assigned mission here, it ultimately becomes totally Blessed by God and becomes totally as one with God's Mighty Eternal Light! You see, Manuana, each soul Light must be absolutely on par with God's Mighty Eternal Light before it can enter Heaven.

And when, at last, the final assigned portion or fraction of God's Laws within Laws, God's Knowledge within Knowledge, and God's Wisdom within Wisdom is learned, digested, and experienced within this sixth Learning Mansion, the soul is then cloaked with God's Mighty Eternal Light. Then gently, and in sweet surrender, the soul is ushered towards an enormous Golden Gate which leads into the Heavenly Realms of Paradise. As the soul gently walks forth with its Heavenly Raiments, Heavenly Thoughts, and Heavenly Wisdom towards this Golden Gate, one can hear Angelical choirs and Heavenly Music from the very core of Heaven itself and from the very core of all the Learning Mansions singing praises to God, our Father, our Creator in Heaven.

A tear of Eternal Joy springs forth from each soul standing in line, head bowed in humility, as the Mighty Gate of Heaven swings wide open! Oh, Manuana, what a sight to behold! When the Mighty Gate of Heaven is opened, each individual soul must pass through a narrow gate, which in ancient times on earth was known as the "eye of a needle." Both within and around this narrow gate is a Light equivalent to the light of your sun. Once a soul passes through this gate, it then has its first eternal glimpse of Heaven. Heaven itself can best be described as one infinite World or Mansion having two inner infinite Worlds or Mansions within it, or as one infinite wheel having two infinite wheels within it. Heaven is situated at the center of all existing universes which are also infinite. For a moment, Manuana, visualize a very large city situated in the center of a vast country on earth. Assume, now, that you are presently within this earthly city. Now, if you stand up and point your hands towards the east and west, visualize your one hand pointed towards the east as reaching out to infinity, and visualize the other hand pointed towards the west as reaching out to infinity. As you have both your hands outstretched to the east and the west, also commence to visualize an infinite beam of light from the north to the south going right through the center of your body. Heaven, too, is at the center of all existing universes. To the east of Heaven, which is the one inner Mansion I speak about, lies infinity with its myriad universes; to the west of Heaven, which includes the other inner Mansion I speak about, lies infinity with its myriad universes as well. Through the center "core" of Heaven is a narrow, infinite beam of Light radiating from the infinite north to the infinite south, which could be considered an infinite "beam zone" between infinite east and infinite west, or an infinite "time zone" between infinite east and infinite west. There is no equation for Heaven's infinity, Manuana, nor for the billions, billions, and more billions of Truths, Sights, and Sounds it has to offer each and every soul. Just knowing that God, the Creator of all Truth and Light, abides here; that His Special Son, Jesus, the King of Light, abides here; that the holy Blessed Virgin Mary abides here; that God's ancient Prophets and Disciples abide here; that God's Special Emissaries abide here, along with a great host of Special Masters, Celestials, and Angels is enough to make each and every soul in Heaven joyous beyond any belief! For a moment or two, Manuana, visualize one of your happiest moments on earth. Now, if you were to augment that one personal experience of happiness by four million times, you then would have some brief idea as to how a soul actually feels in Heaven. Everything a soul sees, hears, or understands in Heaven is total Truth and Pureness! The infinite mountainous ranges, valleys, rivers, streams, and verdure are so rich and pure in vibratory color and Light that a soul, upon entering Heaven, must stand still for a moment or two in order to grasp the immeasurable, intricate beauty it beholds! Every conceivable color and combined color of the spectrum can be seen throughout Heaven. Every flower, every tree, every leaf glitters and shines with its loving peace, harmony, and duty towards God. Even so-called weeds that were or are plucked out from the fields and gardens of Earth or from some similar planet in the Cosmos can be seen here—except that these weeds have now evolved into flowering bushes. Each bush, small or large, has a vast cluster of colorful flowers and leaves on it, and each bush, as well, conveys an aroma that could equal the aromatic smell of a combination of many orchards on your earth plane. Cosmic plant life of infinite sizes and shapes, and Cosmic forests of infinite sizes and shapes abound throughout the infinite wonders of God's Kingdom in Heaven. The unique, colorful forests and plant life are meticulously spread over vast valleys, hills, and mountainous ranges, as they simply glitter and radiate their Eternal joy and beauty to everyone present.

You must also be informed that not only the Plant Kingdom abounds in Heaven, there is also the Animal Kingdom and the Insect Kingdom which dwell here as well. They, too, are an integral part of God's Plan. All animals and insects can cross over, at will, into any area of Heaven but prefer to remain blissfully happy within their own Kingdoms. When they do cross over from time to time, they remain for a brief period and then return to their own Kingdom. There is no such thing as a wild animal or a pesky insect anywhere within God's Kingdom of Heaven. Each and every living Cosmic plant, animal, or insect that withers or dies on earth, or that withers or dies on any other Living Cosmic planet, has earned its rightful place to be in Heaven and to thrive and prosper in God's Eternal Comfort and Peace. Birds crossing from the Animal Kingdom can be seen flying here and there with their sounds of melodious joy, as some animals—three deer, one lion, and one tiger—lie gently within a picturesque field. The sky itself appears to be of a very soft gold-blue-purple, a clear color unlike all the other Learning Mansions, whose skies always appears to be clear, yet blue-purple in color. There is no night in Heaven, nor is there night in any of the previously discussed Learning Mansions. All passageways in Heaven appear to be paved with a warm, soft, cloud-like, spongelike substance quite similar to that seen on only the most highly developed planets within the entire Cosmos. When a soul walks here, it is as though it is walking and floating at the same time. High on a hill, one can see a vast array of pure white-gold buildings which instinctively tell each soul present to "Come forth."

This City of God is of the purest Light, and as the souls come closer and closer to it, they are totally awestruck by the enormity of its beauty, grandeur, and size. Within the center core of this City, which appears to stretch to infinity itself, is a massive, white-gold palatial building whose Light is brighter than all the stars combined in total space. The Heavenly Courtyard is totally awesome, with its finest array of colors and Light, and in many respects it appears as though each new soul, upon its approach to this massive building, is literally walking on myriad, bright, twinkling planets and stars. As souls come closer and closer to this building, they are aware that God, the Creator of Life, is there awaiting their arrival. Upon the direct approach to this magnificent, palace-like building , there are many steps leading upwards to a lengthy landing or another courtyard, before the actual main door to this building is reached. One at a time, each soul now commences to climb these Holy Steps of God. Alongside these Holy Steps, one can see God's Special Emissaries assigned to stand, smile, and inwardly bless each soul as it climbs peacefully and humbly up the Holy Steps towards God.

Now, when the first soul reaches the top of the steps, it commences to walk across the lengthy landing or courtyard until the Mighty Door to this building is reached. When this Mighty Door is reached, it gently opens as each soul, hands clasped in thankfulness and prayer, walks into the glowing, infinite Light within the doorway that beckons them to "Come Forth, My Children."

As the souls walk calmly and peacefully into this building, they are simply overflowing with God's Love and Peace. They continue to walk down a long Light-filled corridor until they reach an enormous door, which gently opens into an enormous Heavenly State Room. Music and Angelical Choirs fill the air within this majestic room as each soul beholds God, the Father of All Life! His Light is brighter than all the combined stars in His Kingdom, and His appearance and countenance is, in truth, like seeing a man filled with all the Love, Truth, Wisdom, Life, and Energy that was, that is, and that will ever be! Manuana, the Purity of God is so Divine and Glorious to behold that each soul present cannot help but literally weep with ecstatic joy as it gently approaches Him, sitting at a distance on His Thronelike Chair. Beside Him stands His Special Son, Jesus, the King of Light, and beside Jesus stands His Mother, the Holy Virgin Mary. As each soul comes face to face with God, they are touched and are blessed by the Mighty Hands of God Himself.

The feeling of actually being touched and blessed by the Hands of God is so totally fulfilling, complete, and overjoyous that each soul present can only give a gentle sigh of total, blessed thankfulness which is fully understood by God. After God's Blessings, each soul is then blessed by the King of Light, who is the Messiah Christ Jesus, and by the Holy Blessed Virgin Mary.

At this time, as well, the newly arrived souls in Heaven will meet other ancient Blessed Beings within God's Kingdom. Some of these ancient Blessed Beings, such as the Messiah's Disciples, the Messiah's earthly father, Joseph, Moses, and a host of other Blessed Beings from planet Earth and from distant galaxies and universes, will mingle and talk to these newly arrived souls in Heaven. It is a day of great rejoicing, for, in truth, these newly arrived Children of God have finally come to their Eternal Father and to their Eternal Home.

After this Heavenly Celebration, each soul is allowed plenty of leisure time to travel throughout God's City and beyond it, if they so choose, or to mingle and talk to whomever they meet or greet in their travels, or some may desire to see their former pets within the Animal Kingdom. You must understand, as well, that there is a great multitude of Holy Cities within God's Kingdom. These cities I speak of are enormous in size and harbor a host of Blessed Beings from all the Cosmos. There is absolutely nothing but Eternal Light, Love, Beauty, Peace, and Harmony within all His Kingdom, and no matter where a soul may wander, there is always something new to discover and behold.

Eventually, each new soul in Heaven will have to fulfill its assignment delegated by the Royal Emissaries of God within the sixth Learning Mansion. Life is constantly being born on earth and on all other universes in the entire Cosmos of Life, and thus, these Heavenly souls must now utilize their official rank as Guardian Angels or utilize some other official rank assigned to them. When a Guardian Angel's assignment, or some other assignment given to an Angel, for example, is completed or fulfilled according to God's Desires, he or she once more returns to Heaven for other Glorified Mansion

Assignments, Cosmic Explorations, Heavenly Learning, and possibly graduating to some newly Edified and Blessed Rank. The indestructible soul continues to grow, prosper, and flourish inwardly throughout Heaven and throughout all its Eternal explorations and Eternal discoveries.

There is no end to God's Miraculous Ways in creating life, as He alone is the Miraculous Seed of All Life and Light that always was, always is, and always will be. Look no further for His beginning Genesis than you would His end Genesis, for, in truth, He is All Life without a beginning and without an end. This factor alone may be very difficult for most people on planet Earth to fathom or grasp until they actually reach Heaven. The earth mind, which is not totally open and functional as it should be at this time, cannot perceive God and infinity as clearly as the Heavenly Mind can and does. Earth minds, Manuana, can basically perceive theoretical beginnings to something within the Cosmos or theoretical endings to something within the Cosmos. The mere concept that God always existed may be much too difficult for most Earth people to even perceive, believe, or uphold. Most people on your planet feel that there has to be a beginning somewhere, simply because everything man sees or everything man does on the planet Earth always appears to have a beginning and always appears to have an end. But not until mankind reaches the Higher Heavenly Vibrations of his intimate soul with God will he commence to understand the true Genesis of God.

And such is the Ultimate Glory of God, His Light, His Wonders, and His Love for All His Dearly Beloved Children in all the Cosmic Universes who were, who are, and who will continue to be, now and forevermore.

7

Reincarnation

Oscar, the theory of reincarnation has been lingering around earth for many centuries. Can you elaborate on this theory, as to whether it is genuinely in league with God? There are some very intelligent, sincere people on this earth plane who believe that they will eventually be reborn to earth in another body after their death. Is there any logic or truth to this matter?

MANUANA, the theory of reincarnation has been lingering on your earth plane for countless centuries simply because the original belief in this theory began in ancient Babylonia. Babylonia was a beautiful, thriving culture at first; then great wickedness, vices, idol worship, and witchcraft became rampant throughout the entire region. Satan and his demons possessed these people and their culture like a plague, and out of this plague, a group of witches and warlock priests created the doctrine of reincarnation. This doctrine, of course, was believed by both lower and wiser beings then, and consequently, this man-made fallacy began to spread both near and far, even to ancient Egypt, ancient India, and eventually around the world. The wickedness in Babylonia grew and flourished until cataclysmic events suddenly ended their culture and civilization.

No, Manuana, the theory of reincarnation is not in league with God, nor has it ever been in league with God, nor will it ever be in league with God! Why would God, in His Wisdom, send his Beloved Children on this side of life back to earth for some supposed previously committed wrongdoing or crime? God does not wish His Children to regress in life by coming back to earth at another time to sin further in another body. Rather, He wishes them to progress in life by working their way towards Heaven, both on earth now and within His Learning Mansions after death. Each person on your earth plane passes earth but once, and each person is blessed with one unique and Eternal soul! Why would God, in His Wisdom, send His Children back to earth without some shred of logical recollection about their so-called past lives? Our Father in Heaven is always loving and forgiving, as He sincerely desires All His Children to be with Him Eternally after death. The soul does not belong to earth and its limited teachings. It belongs to God and His Infinite Teachings. If God desired souls to perpetually return to earth in order to learn some supposed valuable lesson, He would have, in His Wisdom, given each physical being on earth a one-thousand-year life span in which to grow and prosper instead of allowing His Children to die countless times and to be reborn countless times to earth for self-improvement purposes, as believed by many people on your earth plane. But this, as you know, is not God's Plan, nor is the life span on earth one thousand years. God does not wish, at any time, to confuse or to hold back the truth from His Children but constantly desires His Children to seek all truths of life and to be with Him today, tomorrow, and always.

Yes, Manuana, there are literally millions of fantasy tales and untruths that people will create about their so-called past lives, either through their lower conscious imagination; through their lower subconscious imagination; through hypnotism, which is no more than allowing another soul, such as an earthbound soul (a ghost) or a demon soul (one of Satan's assistants), entry into the subconscious mind of the hypnotized individual; or through false or inexperienced psychics, mediums, or mystics who fail to know the true difference between spirit and soul. This so-called earthbound soul or demon soul who temporarily possesses and overshadows an individual's mind, either through hypnotism or through a semi-trance state, can instill many untruths in an individual subjected to it. It can be most convincing, and, unfortunately, most people are deceived by the scenario of past-life rhetoric in these instances. Manuana, there is not one single person on your earth plane today who can truthfully and absolutely verify their supposed past-life experiences. Why? Simply because, in truth, there are absolutely no experiences to verify before the birth of a soul newly assigned to your planet or the birth of a soul newly assigned to any other planet within the entire Cosmic Empire of God. Even I, many centuries ago on earth, was made to believe that we must all reincarnate back to earth many times before our soul was worthy to enter Heaven and to meet God. This I later discovered, upon passing to this side of life, was totally and unequivocally wrong and unfounded!

Manuana, there is a multitude of souls from earth who, upon entering the first Learning Mansion, come to the harsh realization that their belief in reincarnation, according to some of their ancient books, religious scriptures, and dogmas, was totally baseless. Many of these souls become ashamed, traumatized, saddened, and are full of anxieties when they actually discover the real truths behind Satan's earnest wishes for the dispersal of this myth on earth. And, of course, these letdown souls within the first Learning Mansion feel even more traumatized because they accepted this ancient belief at face value instead of doing some serious, intelligent questioning, searches, study, and introspection while on earth and because they failed to recognize the actual "sinful, demonic-possessed originators" of this theory, who once inhabited earth.

In many respects, Manuana, reincarnation beliefs on earth are likened unto "the blind leading the blind," which, to this very day, is still rampant. Satan and his demons do not wish any person happiness on earth, nor do they wish to see anyone progress on earth, but, most importantly, they do not wish anyone to be in league with God and His Truths. This, of course, is why Satan and his demons will impress all types of false beliefs, dogmas, and cults into the minds of man! Consequently, many people believe what they read at face value or believe what someone preaches to them at face value without seriously questioning the written word or the words they hear. Far too often, common myths and superstitions on planet Earth override common sense! But then, again, this is exactly what Satan and his demons desire of man.

There are, sadly, a large number of beings on earth today who write, preach, and indoctrinate others into believing in reincarnation. Fortunately, there are just as many or more beings on earth today who write, preach, and instruct others against the fallacy of reincarnation. The latter group will eventually win out simply because they are in league with the inner truths as to their prime purpose for being on earth and their one and only Eternal soul so assigned to them by God.

Oscar, why do some people believe in reincarnation? What are their motives or aims in this matter? Why are they so intent on believing that countless "past lives" and possible countless "future lives" yet awaiting them on earth could somehow "purify" their souls? Most people on this planet today understand that living on earth is not by any means a bed of roses and can become, on many occasions, a man-made hell through wars, hunger, starvation, privation, prejudices, sinning, and so forth. Why would anyone in their logical thinking ever want to come back to earth in order to be tempted to sin and to experience all types of suffering, heart-aches, and hardships again?

A good percentage of people who do believe in reincarnation are basically intelligent, insecure, sad, or deprived people who, for some reason or other, fail to heed the importance of improving their earthy state, thinking, habits, and actions now or who, sadly, simply resign themselves to their present, earthly, impoverished state by inwardly hoping to someday return to earth as perhaps a maharaja, king or queen, prince or princess, or some other great personage or who hope to return to earth under happier and more prosperous conditions. The vast majority of people adhering to this belief feel that their present, so-called unattainable wishes and unfulfilled desires on earth can be fulfilled within another lifetime on earth.

Bear in mind, as well, that there are an equal number of secure, intelligent, and prosperous people who believe in reincarnation just as emphatically as those previously mentioned. The motives for their beliefs will inevitably vary with each individual person, but the main argument given by some of these more fortunate beings is that they may be somewhat reluctant to give up some of their present luxuries, fame, and fortune during their lifetime and even after death. The inner hope to eventually come back to earth under similar, prosperous conditions is quite prevalent among them. The vast majority of people who do believe in reincarnation might often say that they were a count or duchess in some previous life, that they were a spiritual leader in some temple of Egypt, or that they were Mark Anthony, Cleopatra, or Nefertiti in some past life. Manuana, it would simply astound you how many people on your planet today actually claim to have been Cleopatra or Nefertiti in their past lives! Others will further expound upon their past lives with a host of names, both known and unknown in history, and by so doing, they inwardly feel important not only to themselves but to others around them. The need to express self-importance, or the need to be accepted and recognized in this manner, can and does go beyond the bounds of humility!

Again, the imagination both from the lower conscious level and lower subconscious level leads these people down some mighty frightening pathways in life. A simple untruth in anything cannot and will not bring peace or truth to the heart, mind, and soul of any person on planet Earth. There is, in effect, no true motive or aim to their reincarnation thoughts and beliefs, other than being totally gullible in believing a false doctrine that tends to lead them deeper and deeper into a mire of false thinking, false attitudes, fantasy, and deceit. Those who knowingly praise, preach, or write about the theory of reincarnation, merely assuming that it must be true simply because others believe in it or that because the ancient cultures believed in it, it must be true, or those who knowingly and purposely make up stories about their past lives or about the past lives of others in order to make an impression upon others, or those who purport to be psychics, mediums, or mystics who willfully revel in spreading and expounding upon the past-life scenarios of others and of themselves, will eventually be judged according to their willful and prideful thoughts and actions in these matters. Satan is prideful and deceitful in every way known to man, and he will use and abuse a person mercilessly in order to propagate his many untruths. Satan and his demons celebrate when man wanders off the right path in life for some reason or other or when man tends to believe one of his false doctrines as being a true doctrine of life. Most reincarnationists believe that their past lives were awesome, of high order, or prosperous beyond belief, yet under normal circumstances and according to their theoretical doctrine, their standing on earth today should be even more awesome, more high or prosperous than previously experienced. However, if you were to ask a good percentage of them about their present life conditions on earth today, you might discover that they have not progressed too much from their supposed past-life lessons and experiences but are sadly living in some regressed, repressed, or saddened state of mind and life.

Now, all these messages, Manuana, do not imply that people who honestly and sincerely believe in reincarnation are doomed, bad, or wicked. No. This merely implies that all people on your planet have the God-given right to believe in whatever they so choose, but in choosing a belief, they should also seek the truth and wisdom of this belief with logic and caution. If there are doubts in a belief, then question these doubts profoundly and wisely until the truth within the heart and mind is thoroughly satisfied. However, if there are doubts in a belief and a person still practices a doubtful belief, willfully, openly, and knowingly leading self and others down some wayward path, then it is time to stop, look, and listen to the seriousness of the situation. No good of any kind can come to anyone who purposely leads people astray from the truth of God and His Eternal Light. There were countless wisdoms of Earth that were given and were lost over the centuries, just as there were countless inventions that have come and gone over the centuries. Reincarnation, however, is a sore wound given to man by Satan which, to this very day, continues to fester like a plague from centuries past! It can serve no other purpose than to lead innocent people astray, into believing that they lived on earth many times before and that they supposedly will be given many other chances to find their ultimate love, satisfaction, and purpose in some future earthly life as another person. This simply does not happen! Of the countless soldiers who died miserably in battle in order to save the lives of others throughout history or even in your present day and age, you will not find one of them complaining when they enter the first Learning Mansion. Rather, they are humbly relieved to be as far away from planet Earth as possible, and needless to say, they are overjoyed to know that they will never have to return to suffer, fight, or sin again for any man-made wars, laws, vices, and hardships. And, of course, there are countless people on your planet who have the same profound, positive beliefs and attitudes that any good soldier on this side of life would be willing to share and express.

Humbly, I will say this Truth to all Mankind: you will pass your world but once, so make your life more purposeful, more meaningful, more fulfilling, and as truthful as you can humanly master. Never give up when you are down, nor resign yourself to a defeatist's fate! One day, it will be you and you alone, with your one unique and Eternal soul, who must meet, who must face, and who must ultimately greet your God in Heaven. Take heed to this message: you can hold yourself back in life, both there and here, when you feel Earth's wisdom, lessons, and experiences are far more important, far more valuable, and far more knowledgeable than the Mighty Lessons and Teachings of God within His Mighty Eternal Mansions yet awaiting you.

Can you elaborate on a few earthly experiences that some people claim to be reincarnation-based? What is the explanation for these incidents?

There are many occurrences on Earth that would appear to be reincarnation-based, but, in truth, these occurrences are no more and no less than coincidental, stranger-than-fiction happenings that frequent your planet. Here is one example, Manuana, that many people have experienced on your earth plane. Assume that a parent loses a five-year-old child through death, and assume further that this child is a boy. A year or two after this child's death, the parents give birth to another boy who in many respects not only resembles their lost son but tends to act just like their lost son in certain mannerisms. This does not, in any way, prove that their newborn child is their son who died but merely implies a similarity that tends to perplex them for a while. When their son reaches the age of five, however, they will commence to fully feel, know, and understand that their new son is totally unique and quite different from their deceased son.

Another example: a young boy in India, aged seven, suddenly takes on a different identity and claims to be another person from a village nearby. His parents, who believe in reincarnation, take him to this village in order to verify what he is saying. Everything this young boy said was true, even up to the truth of his knowing the entire family of the house he was guided to. In his trancelike state, he probably has a message or two to reveal to this family, and more than likely under these circumstances, he does. What happens here, Manuana, is that while the young boy was playing leisurely at home, an earthbound soul who is also a male, took possession of his mind and guided him and his parents precisely to where the earthbound soul wished to convey his message. In many respects, it is like a strong semi-trance taking place within the young boy's mind, and the earthbound soul has finally found a way to relay a message of some value or of some importance to his family living in a neighboring village. Once the message is revealed to the earthbound soul's earthly family through this young boy, the earthbound soul is then totally free from being chained down as an earthly ghost. For some reason or other, this earthbound soul was so troubled or traumatized by his sudden death that he refused to enter his Mansion until some message was relayed back to his family. The young boy from the other village was used for that purpose. There is no more and no less of an explanation for this type of occurrence. An hour or two after this occurrence, or in some cases a day or two after this occurrence, the young boy will probably not remember anything at all of this incident. The so-called possession is gone, and he is, once more, free to be his natural self. In any event, it can be deduced that this young boy has psychic or mediumistic talents which he can strive to utilize in life or strive to ignore in life.

Another example is through hypnotism! Many people desire to be hypnotized in order to know more about their supposed past lives. Now, when a person is hypnotized and is regressed back to some so-called "former life-being," a temporal possession by an earthbound soul or by a demon soul takes place within the conscious and subconscious mind of the subject being hypnotized. Unbeknownst to the hypnotized subject and to the hypnotist, this entity silently tempts the open mind of the subject and commences to impress all types of names, dates, and occurrences into the subject's lower conscious and lower subconscious mind state as though the subject was actually remembering or recalling something long ago and far away. You must remember that while all this is happening, the hypnotized person is in a very deep sleep-like state, may feel helpless, and is being strangely subjected to some truths the entity wishes to impart, many half-truths the mind believes, and ultimately, a vast number of lies which the entity thrives on. Now, assume the hypnotized subject claims to have been a John Smith who once lived near London, England, in 1798. Upon further investigation, both the subject and the hypnotist decide to travel to London in order to actually see if there was a John Smith who died in London. Amazingly, they find a gravestone which aptly reads: "JOHN SMITH, BORN 1700, DIED 1798." So, in complete astonishment, both subject and hypnotist automatically decide then and there that reincarnation is a fact of life. But is it? An earthbound soul or a demon soul has much knowledge about death and about graveyards as such and, in the twinkling of an eye, can reveal the names and dates of anyone lying dead in a graveyard anywhere on earth! In some cases, the town or graveyard mentioned is the earthbound soul's or the demon soul's actual burial place!

Some people might aptly maintain that an incident of this order proves the theory of reincarnation or transmigration of souls, whereas some might simply imply that an incident of this order is pure coincidence. It is neither! It is a temporal possession by an earthbound or demon soul attempting to create an illusion of truth, not only to the subject and hypnotist, but to anyone else who wishes to believe what they see or hear at face value. Upon further investigation of other matters revealed to them within this type of hypnotic session, both subject and hypnotist might discover other untruths, which they can gullibly believe in, logically ignore, or unravel.

Then, of course, you have many fraudulent or inexperienced psychics, mediums, or mystics who simply pretend to know a person's past lives. You can quite easily detect these fraudulent or inexperienced individuals by the many inaccuracies they may reveal to you in their psychic readings. If they tend to ask you more questions about yourself and your present problems than they give you answers and solutions to your present life and problems, then you can deduce that they have little or no psychic abilities. If they cannot see who you are today, how can they possibly see who you were a century or two ago? A true psychic, medium, or mystic merely has to see a person, and within an instant, the true past from the time of that person's birth, the true present of that person's life, and the true future of that person's life can be foreseen with phenomenal accuracy. A true psychic, medium, or mystic will never expound about anyone's past lives simply because they know there is absolutely nothing to reveal. Again, I repeat, that true psychics, mediums, or mystics do not advertise their services in any news media but are basically located by word of mouth from people who happen to know of them and their gifts.

There are also some ancient hauntings around your earth plane where some ancient earthbound souls abide. Earthbound souls are basically negative, mischievous souls who can be from the distant past or from more recent times. These souls are biding their time on your earth plane in order to reveal some past mistakes, crimes, or hidden untruths committed while they were on Earth. They actually wish to speak to someone who is able to tune in to their troubled needs and wants. A good psychic, medium, or mystic could tune in to their plight and need, but unfortunately, they are rarely, if ever, asked to do so. These earthbound souls may have committed some so-called perfect murder or some crime or wrongdoing, and they implicitly feel that they must reveal and leave this truth behind on earth forever before they can come to this side of life forever. Upon doing so, they will either be assigned into hell or enter their proper Mansion, whichever applies. These earthbound souls wrongfully feel that if they leave their wrongs behind on earth, then all their crimes or wrongdoings will be forgotten and forgiven on this side of life. The judgment of these souls, of course, rests entirely with God who knows of them and who also knows that sooner or later they must leave their earthly hauntings in order to face His Judgment. Now, Manuana, the important point I wish to bring out here is that, if the theory of reincarnation were true, then surely these ancient earthbound souls would have reincarnated back to Earth many times by now. But this, in truth, is not the case!

And lastly, Manuana, there are these countless ancient and present day books and periodicals which speak so eloquently about reincarnation. Great men, wise men, scholars, philosophers, poets, and ordinary people wrote these books hoping to inspire others, but these books will remain on earth, as there is no place for books of false knowledge, false teachings, or false inspirations anywhere within all the Heavenly Mansions.

8

Meditation

Oscar, what is the main purpose of meditation? What are its benefits? Is it better to meditate alone or with someone else?

THE MAIN PURPOSE of meditation is to strive to find your higher self through positive thoughts, to seek your God through positive thoughts, and, of course, to serve your fellowman through positive thoughts. In simple terms, meditation is just another key to soul development. This soul development can bring a person closer to the realities of the Christ Light and Mind which everyone is latently blessed with on your earth plane. Unfortunately, not everyone on your earth plane is willing to sacrifice some of their time in order to find this Truth and reality so imbedded within the soul. To seek the truth in self, in God, and in others is to quietly sit down and to peacefully think kind thoughts towards one's fellowman. Please bear in mind, as well, that meditation is not only an individualistic cleansing process of the heart, mind, and soul, but can, on many occasions, be considered a healing process of self in serving others. True meditation is totally giving or sharing one's kindly thoughts towards God and mankind, whereas prayer is asking God for guidance and assistance and, of course, sharing one's thoughts towards God and mankind.

Manuana, the benefits of meditation can be most fulfilling, providing those who practice and partake in this beneficial action use their inner meditative gains both lovingly and wisely. To be able to find yourself, to be able to understand

85

God's Ways a little better, and to know inwardly that your meditation has somehow assisted someone, somewhere is an infinite blessing in itself! People who meditate properly and lovingly do prosper within their daily lives simply because they have unlocked a valuable door in assisting others, they have discovered a valuable truth in seeking God, and, lastly, they commence to perceive a valuable intuitive gift within themselves. The simple truth is this: in assisting your fellowman with positive, meditative wishes of the heart, mind, and soul, you have automatically pleased and served God in the same manner. When a person pleases and serves God in some manner on your earth plane, you can be assured that some blessings and rewards will be forthcoming.

Now, it does not matter whether a person meditates alone or with a group of people. Some people on your earth plane prefer to meditate alone, whereas some people prefer to meditate with a group of positive-minded individuals in order to serve and help others as a rescue group. In both instances positive results can be achieved.

Oscar, what is the correct procedure to begin meditation? Also, what things should a person guard against when meditating?

To commence meditation at any time a person must sincerely want to meditate. At no time should a person meditate thinking, or assuming, meditation is a daily or weekly, mundane chore or a mundane, mind-consuming duty. At no time should a person meditate in a lazy or unwilling manner or feel that the time spent for meditation could be used for better purposes somewhere else. At no time should a person meditate for evil or wicked purposes, for these thoughts and visualizations will truly backfire! No one should meditate when he is overly tired or when he is overly troubled. When a person is tired, then sleep is in order; when a person is troubled, then a prayer to God for peace and comfort is in order. Remember, true meditation is not thinking about self while meditating, but, rather, thinking kindly and thoughtfully about one's fellowman. In meditation, for example, think kindly about the poor people around your world so that they might have food, clothing, and other necessities which you, perhaps, take for granted; think kindly about sickly and hospitalized people around your world in the good hopes and wishes that they will be ultimately guided, assisted, and cured; think kindly about abused children and abused adults on your planet who need love, guidance, and protection; think kindly about crime victims so that they might be given the insight and strength to forgive those who have done them wrong; think kindly about your loved ones, family, friends, acquaintances, enemies, and about all other things in life which you feel need assistance, guidance, or repair. Remember this well: do not think about yourself while you meditate.

Meditate for a period of three to four minutes a day or a week, and no more! This is emphatically suggested, Manuana, simply because most people who meditate for extremely long periods of time tend to think more about their own needs rather than the needs of others. Also, many people who meditate to extremes tend to become unruly, edgy, illogical, unrealistic, and can, in some instances, create an insane view of what should be life's normal, daily realities. By meditating for only three to four minutes a day or a week at first, a person can quite readily concentrate upon the needs of others rather than upon one's own personal needs. It is by giving that a person will eventually receive. But, note as well, that in meditating, a person should never meditate for the purpose of receiving anything in return. Those who meditate should just meditate for the sole purpose of giving or sharing good thought-wishes towards their fellowman. Simply understand that God chooses His Moment, His Hour, and His Day to reward His Children whenever they please Him. And, of course, true meditation does please Him!

Now, always try to meditate in peaceful surroundings, be it alone or with a group of people. Do not meditate with anyone you feel uncomfortable with; if you do, always strive to mend your differences with this individual before you commence to meditate. Meditation, in many respects, is a form of inner love which you are intending to express towards your fellowman. There is no room for hate, jealousy, envy, pride, greed, gossip, mockery, or for anything else that might be considered negative when you meditate. Find a comfortable sitting position, make no unruly sounds, then commence to meditate in silence. As you know, Manuana, there are many types of meditation practices on your earth plane, but the simplest method of sitting quietly and peacefully alone or with a group of people is by far the best method in achieving positive results. Do not meditate beyond the three to four minute time span until you are mentally, physically, and spiritually prepared to do so! When you honestly feel that you are ready to meditate for longer periods of time, then you can expand the time for meditation to one half hour once a week, and then eventually to one hour earth time *once a week* and *no more!* Going beyond this absolute time limit can be dangerous and can create unnecessary and unforeseen mental problems for an individual. It may even create a mental breakdown as some people have sadly discovered and experienced on earth.

Remember at all times that you are presently on earth and that you should always have your feet firmly planted on earth while you are there. Do not become obsessed or possessed with meditation nor with anything else on earth, nor feel that meditation will open all earthly doors to you, when, in fact, it will not, nor feel that meditation will give you some great earthly powers, when, in fact, it will not. If you are not prepared or equipped to meditate, then you would be far better off doing something else more in harmony with your personality and time. If you honestly feel that you are mentally and spiritually equipped to meditate, then do so with humility, common sense, and wisdom!

Oscar, prayer serves a great purpose for the mind and soul of an individual. There are many benefits in prayer, but some people complain that their prayers or belief in God has not really assisted them in life. Is there any basis for their complaints?

We both know the value and great purpose of prayer. It assists the mind, the soul, and the well-being of an individual.

A memorized, written prayer to God is very beneficial, whole-some, and worthy. However, He does request those simple and humble outpourings of the mind and heart from each individual on earth before or after a written prayer is uttered. Say a prayer to God as though you were actually talking to Him. Sing with Him, laugh with Him, cry with Him, discuss any matter with Him—but "be" with Him in your prayers! A memorized, written prayer is both inspiring and acceptable to God, but do not forget to communicate to God on a more intimate, more personal Father-son, Father-daughter basis. He loves you and He cares about you for He is your True Father in Heaven! Come to God with your personal prayers and your personal discussions as a child might do, with total innocence, belief, clearness, and truth. Make your many requests to Him as you would to your earthly parents, your spouse, your dearest friends, or whomever you happen to love and trust, and believe with all your soul that He will answer you. He does hear all prayers, but sometimes the prayer requests may be overly selfish, immature, or far too premature to be granted instantly.

Sometimes a person prays for a person or two so that they might improve their ways, yet there does not appear to be any great or even minor changes seen or forthcoming. Why? Simply because the person who prays must understand that wayward people do not necessarily change overnight—espe-cially if they are unwilling to listen to sound reason or if they simply refuse to pray and believe in God and in His Many Miracles. Nonetheless, a wayward person can still change in due time—after a series of personal blunders and mistakes have been made, recognized, and ultimately rectified. In some cases, unfortunately, some wayward people on your earth plane will simply never change until they reach this side of life.

Sometimes a person prays for an improvement in a loved one or another person, only to eventually realize that the change requested should be more self-directed. The attitude of a loved one or of another person may never change, but the attitude of the person who prays should change in order to be free of this wayward person while on earth or to simply accept and tolerate the wayward person as he is. Nonetheless, a prayer should still be said for all wayward people in spite of their inherent attitudes and actions on earth.

Sometimes a person prays for personal happiness, good luck, or for some form of earthly wealth but fails to receive an immediate answer. God hears this prayer, but in His Wisdom, He knows His Children implicitly well—far better than they know themselves. He knows those who are instantly deserving and those who must faithfully wait, persevere, and believe in His Will and His Time. If God granted all prayerful requests instantly and without foresight, your world would tend to become totally uncaring and totally disordered and selfish! Those beings who are disappointed in God, or who claim their prayers have not been answered, simply do not have the patience, insight, and foresight to wait for their true answer from Him. There are millions and millions of prayerful requests that God grants to His Children on earth on a daily basis, but there are just as many prayerful requests from His Children on earth who must faithfully wait for another time.

Take note, as well, that some prayers may never be granted at all due to some underlying negative motives within the person who said the prayer or within the requested prayer itself. God simply cannot be deceived! God knows what is good or bad for All His Children on earth. Unfortunately, many of His Children on earth are much too impatient, unthinking, and uncaring to recognize this one Truth about His Patience with them, His Thinking of them, and His Caring for them. So many times people pray for the wrong things, assuming that what they prayed for was right, just, and deserving. They act upon this prayer themselves instead of waiting a day or two, a week or two, or a month or two to think things over seriously and sensibly. Sadly, and much later on, they regret their impetuous actions with anguish, pain, and suffering for not having listened to the inner voice within them which urged them to "Wait!"

A prayer is a direct communication line between you and God. When you pray, pray humbly, faithfully, and sincerely, and be willing to wait for His Answer! The answer may come through a loved one, a friend, an acquaintance, a letter, a telegram, a telephone call, some coincidental advice given to you from a complete stranger, a dream, an overpowering intuitive feeling you may have, or someone else might have, concerning your prayer's wish or request, a poignant passage you may be reading from a book, some impressive words from a song you might be hearing now or very shortly, or simply from a host of other sources God may decide to work through. Be patient in all things, and you will ultimately experience the intimate rewards and miracles of true prayer. God wants all His Children to be happy and to prosper in life, but He does desire complete love, truth, and patience from His Children at all times so that His Will for them through prayer and His Wisdom for them through prayer can be fulfilled.

There are so many vast, personal benefits in saying a prayer and in meditating. Why are so many people on earth reluctant to better themselves through prayer and meditation?

Manuana, if each person on your earth plane prayed to God with total love, trust, and sincerity and if each person on your earth plane prayed and meditated to assist mankind, you would commence to see a great transformation towards peace and understanding around planet Earth. But as you know, each person and each country on your earth plane is uniquely different in their thoughts, beliefs, and actions, and will continue to be this way until the One Church of Life, which is God Himself, commences to bring forth the oneness of love and understanding to every soul upon your planet and to every country upon your planet. The King of Light, the Messiah Jesus Christ, will return to earth with His Heavenly Ambassadors and Counselors, and when He does, the world will finally commence to fully comprehend the true oneness of worshipping and respecting His Father according to His Father's Laws, Rules, and Regulations—not according to man's laws, rules, and regulations.

Do not forsake this truth, for the prophecies of old will be fulfilled so that, at last, earth will find its peace; so that, at last, the meek will inherit the earth; so that, at last, peace, harmony, and love will be on earth "as it is in Heaven." There have been and still are "holy" wars upon your planet which are foolishly being fought; there have been and still are Holy Rules upon your planet which are being ignored; there have been and still are "holy" churches upon your planet that fail to practice what they preach or that tend to be envious of other church denominations or that practice self-righteous teachings; there have been and still are innocent people who are slaughtered for their religious, political, or social beliefs; and, lastly, there have been and still are innocent people being slaughtered, condemned, or ignored because of their color, race, or creed. All these sad earthly actions are so demeaning to God and to His Universal Teachings of Love and Understanding that He still must look upon mankind on earth as being primitive in spite of his so-called wisdom and modern-day technology. There is no wisdom in war; there is no wisdom in ignoring The Ten Commandments of God; there is no wisdom in churches fighting one another nor in maintaining that *their* beliefs and rules are the only true source or true road to God; nor is there any wisdom in slaughtering innocent people for their religious, political, or social beliefs; nor is there any wisdom in slaughtering, condemning, or ignoring innocent people because of their color, race, or creed. All that God desires of All His Children on earth is for them to love one another, accept one another, harmonize with one another, and ultimately work with one another in His Love!

Why are there so many people on earth reluctant to better themselves through prayer and meditation? This question alone may involve millions of answers from just as many millions of people on your earth plane. However, some reasons for one's reluctance to pray or meditate could be that a person has an uncaring or wayward attitude about life, is spiritually ignorant, has had a traumatic upbringing, is being abused in some manner, has been severely indoctrinated in religion and has, in retaliation, chosen to go to the other extreme, or has adopted a series of self-pitying ideas and concepts about life which primarily incorporate personal grudges and hate. It is so unfortunate, Manuana, that mankind will not totally harmonize in true prayer for peace, health, and prosperity nor in true meditation for inner love and understanding. There are, nonetheless, millions of people around your world today who do strive for peace and harmony through prayer, through meditation, and through their positive actions. These beings are to be praised for their sincerity, for their diligent efforts, and for their peacemaking attempts. God truly knows them and truly loves them as they serve Him!

One day, when the world least expects it to happen, the King of Light, the Master and Lord Jesus Christ, will return to earth with His Heavenly Ambassadors and Counselors so assigned by His Father. He will finally rectify man's confusion about life and transform man's attitudes through His Father's True Light, Love, and Wisdom! Peace, love, and understanding will come.

9

Mediumship

There are two types of mediums on earth: the mental medium and the physical medium. Oscar, will you please elaborate on them? Also, how can a person distinguish between a genuine medium and a false medium?

M ANY PEOPLE on your earth plane are born with psychic or mediumistic talents but tend to lose this inner capability as they grow up due to man-made fears and man-made beliefs and disbeliefs. For example, when a young girl sees something unusual, such as a friendly soul or a soul playmate from this side of life, her parents will more than likely dismiss this matter as being totally ridiculous because *they* did not see someone, or they simply maintain that their daughter has a very imaginative mind. No. Their child did not imagine this truth, for rarely will a child attempt to deceive a parent in matters involving this so-called earthly phenomenon. How could a child possibly deceive a parent in matters of this order, when, in truth, this so-called phenomenon is just as unusual, exciting, and shocking to a child as it might be to a good and loving parent? A young, innocent child can be far more psychically perceptive than a parent. Why is this so? Well, the child's mind has not yet been conditioned to doubt or to scoff at everything seen or heard on a sixth-sense level of mind. Unfortunately, the parent ultimately discourages the child from pursuing anything and everything that might be re-motely considered phenomenalistic. Consequently, the inner talents of mediumship will eventually dissipate from this child's mind and soul due to the parents' doubts, disbeliefs, and fears. Most parents raise their children to tell the truth, but when the truth of their child is denied—can you imagine how their child must feel? The child, of course, is devastated and, sadly, has no recourse but to heed his parents' advice and discouragement.

There are, however, unusual cases where a child tends to ignore the advice and discouragement of a parent and secretly accepts phenomenal sights and sounds as being a simple, natural way of life. Hence, this child will not lose this talent or gift but will grow up with it. Take into account, as well, that there are many parents who do believe in life beyond the grave and who do not discourage their children from talking about the unusual sights and sounds they may perchance see and hear in their growing up years. Again, these children will mature and prosper with their intuitive insights and abilities. They will not fear death for, in some cases, they will have seen a soul or two from this side of life, and they will not fear life for, in some cases, they will have been given some philosophic truths from this side of life as well. Manuana, anyone on your earth plane who has actually seen a departed soul from this side of life, or who has had some "out of body" death experience, automatically dispels death as being no more and no less than a man-made myth! The physical body of an individual is left behind on earth after death but not the Eternal soul, which is made in God's image! The Eternal soul, as you know, must work its way to God in Heaven as previously mentioned.

Now, the mental mediumship, or mind mediumship as it is sometimes called, is by far the most superior type of mediumship on your earth plane. Those who are blessed with this type of mediumship are simply born this way. Their mind, heart, and soul are quite naturally attuned to the Godhead of Life from birth. As they grow and mature, they sense an urgency to humbly share their true gifts of prophecy, clairaudience, clairvoyance, and healings with those around them and with the world if assigned to do so. People in this league are considered prophets or saints on this side of life but are rarely given this distinction on your earth plane. You can detect them now and again "by their profound truths and miraculous works." They are attuned to phenomenal sights and sounds to a great degree—for being attuned to the Godhead of Life will allow this type of medium to mind-travel or soul-travel to many vast reaches of their Universe until they ultimately find the truth they seek. They can mind-travel or soul-travel into the past, the present, and deep into the future. In many instances, you might consider this type of medium to be a type of "reporter of truth" who more than willingly shares prophetic insights with others and, in some cases, with the world. The mental or mind medium can go into a trance state from time to time but is not allowed to flaunt this state of attunement in order to publicly prove that there is life beyond death, or for some type of public exhibition in order to gain prestige or fortune, or for seeking notoriety in some public media. They are mentally and spiritually equipped to handle their public quite naturally and openly without having to go into a trance state! They are not assigned to prove their worth to anyone on earth—except to fulfill their purposes on earth with truth! For those who can see beyond the veil of earthly life, then let them see. For those who can hear beyond the veil of earthly life, then let them hear. For those who cannot see or hear beyond the veil of earthly life, yet still faithfully believe in sixth-sense truths, then humbly, they are blessed with having great insight!

Whenever a true medium goes into a trance state, it must be extremely private and timely, and only a few select people may be present. Those truly gifted in this way will understand this latter statement more than anyone else! In the above mentioned message, Manuana, I am not referring to the inexperienced or fraudulent mediums who claim to be mental or mind mediums. The true mental or mind mediums mainly channel their chief guide, a higher being assigned to them on earth, but can, on occasion, channel some other higher being assigned to them for a moment or two, or, at times, can channel a loving soul from the first, second, or third Learning Mansion for a moment or two. Anyone who claims to do otherwise is inexperienced in these matters or is deceptive or fraudulent in these matters. All chief guides, as you already know, Manuana, are ancient beings who have already reached Heaven and who have been assigned to help their earthly protégés. Chief guides are not recently deceased relatives, friends, or acquaintances, nor are they some prominent or ordinary beings back from the seventeenth, eighteenth, or nineteenth century! So, in effect, if any medium claims that his chief guide is a recently deceased aunt or uncle, friend, or acquaintance, or that his chief guide is some deceased prominent or ordinary figure from the eleventh century up to and including your present century, then doubts are in order. If a medium claims to be channeling Jesus, the King of Light, the Virgin Mary, Joseph, Moses, or a host of other Heavenly Beings known to earth, then you can be more than certain that deceit and fraud are involved! These Heavenly Beings of the Highest Order are never channeled through any medium, at any time, nor will this ever be! If Jesus decides to see someone on your earth plane for some special purposes, then He will make His Appearance and His Wisdom clearly known to whomever He chooses, and the same applies to the Virgin Mary and to the host of other Holy Edified Beings from the Heavenly Kingdom of God.

Each soul on your planet is assigned a Guardian Angel, and it is one's Guardian Angel who is, in effect, one's true and only assigned chief guide. The true mental mediums or mind mediums are born to serve mankind wisely, not foolishly! They do not knock on anyone's door in order to flaunt their services but wisely understand that people must seek them out. The true mental medium or mind medium can basically see, hear, and communicate with souls from the first, second, and sometimes from the third Learning Mansion. They basically cannot see or communicate with any developing souls beyond the third Learning Mansion unless assigned to do so. They are, nonetheless, able to communicate with their Heavenly Guide at all times, yet are very rarely privileged to see them. The basic communication with a Guardian Angel is channeled through the right side of the brain, through their right prophetic ear, through symbols, and through direct, clearly defined visions. Very often all three methods are employed simultaneously so that, in many respects, many truths are deciphered simultaneously. If a medium claims to be directly communicating with God Himself, or to be channeling God through a trance state, then deceit is definitely being practiced. God does not communicate with His Children in this direct manner, nor is it necessary for Him, at any time, to come through a person in a trance state! He communicates with His Children through His Guardian Angels—assigned to each and every one of them on earth—through individual faith and prayer, through silent meditation, and, of course, through loving and serving one's fellowman.

Manuana, common sense must always prevail when someone seeks and consults a medium. If the medium is truthful about you and your life, then you know the medium is of good order. But if the medium is wrong about you and your life, then you know that the medium is not of good order. If the medium expounds upon reincarnation, negative thoughts and ideas, promises you wealth and glory on earth for great sums of money, or does anything that might be considered false and unwise, then think twice about believing what you hear and what you see. There are many inexperienced mediums, or channelers as some might call themselves, on your earth plane today. These inexperienced mediums fail to test the entities coming through them, merely assuming that they are who they claim to be. If their supposed guides or entities tell them half-truths, are very difficult to comprehend, are blasphemous on occasion, or simply impart false information, then you can be sure that the medium is attuned to an earthbound soul (a ghost) or to a demon soul (one of Satan's assistants). These inexperienced mediums or channelers are not ready to teach, to show, or to prove anything to anyone on your earth plane. It may take years of prayer, meditation, and attunement before these inexperienced mediums become worthy to serve God and to serve their fellowman. Then, of course, there are also the fraudulent charlatans who merely pretend to be mediums for monetary purposes, for notoriety, and for deceitful purposes! These individuals are generally discovered sooner or later, but God knows who they are!

Now, physical mediumship, as opposed to mental or mind mediumship, can, through personal sight or photography, give everyone a glimpse or two of a departed soul from this side of life. Many true and documented photographs have been taken of souls who have actually materialized with the assistance of a rare but true physical medium on your earth plane. But there are just as many false sightings and false photographs of supposed materialized souls. These are, in truth, no more than a fraudulent performance by charlatans who call themselves physical mediums. Their tricks to deceive mankind could equal the tricks of a shrewd magician. These charlatans often use a Ouija board; practice table tipping; hire a friend or two to don white florescent sheets against a black painted background in order to create a ghostly effect or two; use all types of gadgetry and sound systems to create wind noises and shrilling, haunting sounds; and, sadly, their schemes go on and on. These earthly troublemakers can show no truths with their negative actions and instruments to anyone seeking some positive proof of life beyond death. Rather, they work against actual, positive proofs in these matters. Innocent people are deceived into believing that what they see and hear is real, when, in reality, this is not so. Sooner or later these charlatans will be discovered and exposed, but the damage is done! Hence, many innocent people compound their disbeliefs already formulated about mediums and commence to believe that life after death must also be false or a hoax.

Normally, true physical mediums are born to different parts of your earth plane in order to give some sound evidence of life's continuance beyond the grave. The proof they can give to earth is real and outstanding, but it is unfortunate that so many charlatans in this field confuse mankind with their base and false enactments of departed life. A true physical medium is attuned to God and can, in many respects, teach mankind many phenomenal truths about life on earth and about life after death. Yet, when true physical mediums come along, they are often rigorously tested, ridiculed, and disbelieved by those who feel all physical mediums or all mediums are deceivers! This, of course, is just not so! In simple terms, Manuana, it is the mediumistic charlatans, it is the inexperience of some scientific testers who formulate their sixth-sense theories with hasty prejudgments and conclusions, and, lastly, it is the cumulation of some man-made religious teachings which have persistently made it difficult for some of God's Truths from this side of life to finally be decoded and shared with sincere, seeking people on earth. There are some true physical mediums on your earth plane now who are staying out of the limelight completely but who, nonetheless, have true documented files about their mediumistic feats. Upon their deaths, the truth will come forth in a documented book or two, thus showing mankind some of the simple truths, materializations, and symbols of life he so stubbornly refuses to believe. When God grants a newborn soul a gift or talent, He expects His Gifts and His Talents to be used sincerely and wisely. This you will find among the rare but true mental mediums and among the rare but true physical mediums on your earth plane.

Oscar, is it dangerous for mediums gifted primarily in the area of prophecy to attempt exorcisms, or for mediums gifted primarily in healing to give readings? Was Jesus mediumistic, and, if so, why are so many people reluctant to accept this fact?

Manuana, all true mediums should know their spiritual and earthly limits, talents, and gifts. All true mediums should be willing to share their truths with their fellowman but should always be aware that they are human and that they can make earthly errors and mistakes just like anyone else. They are not infallible, nor is anyone else on earth infallible. Some mediums are blessed with gifts of clairvoyance, clairaudience, prophecy, prediction, and healing, whereas some might be more blessed in the areas of psychometry, extrasensory perceptions, and possibly exorcisms. Others may be more attuned to the soul by reading auras and symbols, going into trance, and so forth. Mediums are uniquely gifted or talented but must, nonetheless, always strive to develop and perfect their own abilities in a positive way, and must also strive to serve God and their fellowman in a positive way.

Many of the ancient prophets and saints were mediumistic. Jesus, the King of Light, was also mediumistic. He was the exception to all the rules of mediumship on your earth plane in that He was completely gifted in these matters. His Light, His Truth, His Pureness, and His Infallibility cannot and will not be equaled by anyone else on planet Earth! Nonetheless, all true mediums on your earth plane today must respect the gifts within them and should always strive towards attaining the Christ Mind as best they can, to serve their fellowman as best they can, and to fulfill their purpose in God's Plan and Directives as best they can. There is absolutely no room for any true medium to be prideful or greedy, or to harbor personal hatreds or vendettas. And, of course, Manu-ana, a true mental or mind medium, or a physical medium, should never have to prove his worth to anyone on your earth plane, either privately or publicly, but should be equipped to face and to handle the public calmly, naturally, and wisely at all times. If his work is just and sincere, and he is, in all truth, revealing some of God's Joys and Wonders, then who on earth could possibly be against him?

The vast majority of people on your earth plane are practical-minded and do not necessarily believe in mediumistic matters. They have been indoctrinated into believing that all mediumistic matters are evil and not in keeping with God and His Laws. Oddly, though, their religious teachings are full of wondrous prophecies, beliefs, and sayings which emanated from gifted, mediumistic individuals—including the greatest Prophet and Master of all time: Jesus, the King of Light. It is unfortunate that those opposed to mediumship-based truths in your present day and age are those earthbound minds and disbelievers who have much to learn about their own inner weaknesses, fears, and false man-made beliefs; those who are fearful that God will be offended with them if they believe in the unknown or in the unseen facets of life; and, lastly, those who are unwilling to admit that there is more to Heaven and earth than their human understanding is willing to accept, to learn, and to cherish. There is nothing on earth and there is nothing in Heaven that God does not want His Children to know—for in all His Love and in all His Wisdom, He created His Children to freely seek and to freely find His Truths in all things.

Oscar, there are many areas of mediumship: prophecy and predictions, mental telepathy, exorcisms, psychometry, speaking in tongues, ESP, reading auras and symbols, clairvoyance, and clairaudience. Will you elaborate on some of these areas?

Many well-informed parapsychologists and other mediumship investigators on your earth plane have already sifted through, defined, and ultimately explained many of the above mentioned areas of mediumship. Many of these same parapsychologists and investigators have written about these areas of mediumship either in a trusting manner or in a disbelieving manner. Nonetheless, I wish to emphatically state that these areas of mediumistic phenomena do exist on planet Earth. Whether they are believed or disbelieved is of no importance.

There is one area I wish to discuss first and that is the area of speaking in tongues. When I communicate to you, Manu-ana, I am communicating to you in a language which you thoroughly understand. It would be totally futile for me to communicate to you in a language which you do not understand. No true medium, in a trance state, will ever speak to a person in another language unless the language is totally understood by the person seeking guidance or help. A chief guide is basically assigned to speak through the medium in a language both used and known by the medium. There are occasions, however, when a true medium can speak a foreign language known to those present, but not all mediums are gifted in this manner. Also note that an inexperienced or a fraudulent medium might attempt speaking in "tongue gibberish" within a trance state in order to impress others.

Now, many centuries ago when Jesus told His Disciples to travel far and near to spread the Word of God, He did tell them that "your tongues will be as one with everyone whom you meet within your travels." In other words, Manuana, whomever they met, the disciples were instantly gifted and knowledgeable about the other's earthly language. They could coherently speak another man's earthly language at any time, any place, and any hour. Hence, these disciples spread the Word of God both far and near without experiencing any language barriers. It is truly that simple! God did not bestow upon them a language of "tongue gibberish" but rather gave them a gift of speaking many earthly languages spoken in many lands beyond Israel. Yet, today on your earth plane, there are many people who actually believe that "tongue gibberish" is the mysterious language of God! No. This is not the mysterious language of God, nor will this ever be the mysterious language of God! If God has a message to reveal to anyone on your earth plane, it will be clear, concise, and coherent. God does not desire His Children to be confused about any matters concerning Him but does desire His Children to use good, sensible judgment in the many man-made rituals they believe in and practice.

Now, in regard to all the other talents of mediumship you mentioned, Manuana, using these gifts wisely will allow any true medium to flourish and prosper. Some mediums are more gifted in some areas than others simply because they are born this way. But again, I must reiterate, that it is the mediums' responsibility to thoroughly know, to thoroughly understand, and to ultimately share their gifts with their fellowman—providing they are ready to do so. If a medium is not ready to help others for some reason or other, or is inexperienced in areas of mediumship even though he feels otherwise, then caution and waiting is in order. An inexperienced medium may become a true medium in time, but this may take many years of meditation, prayer, and a deep willingness to serve one's fellowman humbly and wisely.

Oscar, what is the best procedure for conducting and taking part in a séance? How can people avoid fraudulent séances and mediums? What are the benefits of holding séances?

A séance should be no more and no less than one hour's duration of meditation, should consist of a group of level-headed, soul-searching individuals, and should always have a reputable, true medium present. A séance can be held once a month providing those present are sincerely willing to meditate and are willing to sincerely learn more about life's hidden mysteries. If the medium goes into trance during a séance, then listen intently to the messages coming through. If the medium does not go into a trance state during each séance session, do not be disappointed but, rather, be grateful in knowing that your meditation has assisted someone, somewhere, during your hour of giving. Normally, the people present at a séance arrange their chairs in a circle. The true medium, who sits among these people, should always be able to move about in the event that a trance state takes place. Sometimes the medium must stand in front of an individual or behind an individual when messages from this side of life are given, or, in some cases, the medium merely remains seated when messages are given. The room itself should be peaceful and unlit—for it is within a darkened room that lights around people, or auras around people, may be seen. And, on occasion, souls from this side of life may be seen for those prepared to see them. Always bear in mind that a séance is just another way of developing one's level of awareness and attunement in life. Say a quiet, sincere prayer before the séance begins, then commence to meditate silently in the dark.

If a medium is unbearably rude, chatty, pompous, high-strung, or fidgety, or becomes unusually melodramatic before, during, or after a séance, then something is not in order. If a medium uses a Ouija board, uses a crystal ball, reads palms, practices table tipping, or does anything else that might be considered unbecoming a true soul-searching individual during a séance, or does something that is not in keeping with safe, sincere practices of meditation, then something is not in order. If a medium, in a trance state, harshly scolds or lectures anyone present during a séance, then something is not in order. If a medium, in a trance state, tends to be farfetched, blasphemous, shrieks, starts prancing all over the place, or does other things that appear totally ridiculous or unsound to one's better judgment and common sense, then something is not in order. If a medium is reputable and true, then none of the above mentioned negative actions will take place!

The pure intent of a true séance as opposed to a fraudulent séance is still vastly misunderstood by millions of people on your earth plane. Unfortunately, most people are inclined to believe only the horror stories and inaccuracies associated with fraudulent séances. They simply cannot fathom or believe that positive séances are in league with this side of life and are in total harmony with God! The media, whether written or seen, has adopted some fearsome, horrific attitudes towards anyone associated with séances. No true medium can at any time, or does at any time, conjure souls from this side of life in order to entertain or pacify someone on earth! However, many inexperienced and fraudulent mediums have certainly attempted to do so in deceptive ways! When the voice of a soul comes through a medium in a trance state from the first Learning Mansion, as an example, it is not because the true medium conjures that soul's voice to come through. No. Not at all! It is because that soul's voice is assigned to come through the medium by the medium's chief guide. This soul's voice does not come back to earth for some evil purposes but merely wishes to relay a peaceful, loving message or two to someone present at the séance who can and will recognize that voice. After the soul's voice has finished its message through the medium, the chief guide once more takes over. When a soul from this side of life is actually seen by people at a true séance, it is not because this soul was conjured by the medium or by those present. Not at all! It is because this soul was assigned to appear in full view as directed by the medium's chief guide.

The benefits of a séance, of course, are to help your fellowman through meditation, to learn more about life beyond death through a true medium's chief guide, and, lastly, to become more aware of and attuned to one's own chief guide, one's Guardian Angel.

10

Spiritual Healing

How can a person become a "spiritual healer" on earth? Why are there so few spiritual healers?

THERE ARE NO ACTUAL STEPS in becoming a spiritual healer on earth, Manuana, for in all respects the vast majority of people on your earth plane are born healers but fail to realize this one vital truth about themselves. True psychics, mediums, and mystics certainly know of their healing potential, and, of course, so do some other individuals blessed with the gift of spiritual healing. Those who do practice spiritual healings alone or charismatically have had excellent results and many testimonials to their credit. Most people on your planet have experienced "hot" or "burning" hands from time to time. When this takes place, the healing forces or energies come through the subconscious mind from the inner soul of an individual. The subconscious mind then releases this force or energy into the conscious mind, which subsequently releases it into a person's hands and fingers. The fingers then act as the electrical healing antennas of the soul. This healing force from the soul is always attuned to God, so whenever one's hands tend to be extremely "hot," a person can actually commence to self heal or group heal. The effects and ultimate proof of this type of miraculous healing can be most gratifying to both the healer and to the recipient. Most people who practice spiritual healing have been made aware of their inner talents from birth and simply continued to nourish and develop them, both frequently and wisely. The more one practices spiritual healings, such as in the laying on of hands (touching self or another person for better health) or in absence healing (meditating and praying for a person's better health), the greater one's ability to heal becomes.

In extremely ancient times, this form of healing was very commonplace in such areas known today as the Middle East, China, North America, South America, and, of course, on many other inhabited islands scattered here and there around your world. Each person could heal self and others as well. One's inner faith was attuned to self, to nature, and to the infrequent visits from the Celestials of Light who were commonly known as the "gods from the stars." It was these Celestials of Light who actually taught ancient peoples of earth the processes of self healing and group healing. It was also these Celestials of Light who once taught man on earth how to use herbal plants and roots for natural healings, and it was also these Celestials of Light who once taught mankind on earth a host of other vital, civilizing facts such as language, agriculture, mathematics, universal laws, art, and so much more. Once this healing knowledge was known on earth, it was practiced frequently, humbly, and wisely by its peoples. The miracles of ancient spiritual healings are no different from modern day miracles of spiritual healings. In those days, Manuana, people had no qualms or fears about believing in themselves and in nature. Their lives were not as complex nor as busy as some people on planet Earth profess to be today, however. Now, if they were fearful or prideful in any manner, they could not be healed. Whenever this did happen, they were advised by their elders to settle their thoughts near a stream, river, lake, or forest. Once this was accomplished, they were healed! Absolute trust in one's ability to heal self or to be healed by someone else, absolute humility in self and in serving others, and absolute faith in life's miraculous ways were and continue to be those vital factors essential for spiritual healings to actually work.

There are some people on your earth plane today who do practice their God-given spiritual healing talents on others with no more and no less than miraculous results! But why just some people? The simple truth is that most people on your earth plane are not even remotely aware of their hidden ability to heal; are not willing to seek this truth about themselves even if they did know; are more inclined to believe in modern day methods of medical healing; or are total disbelievers in spiritual healers and healings for one reason or another. As I mentioned before, Manuana, most people on your earth plane have the potential to heal themselves or someone else if they made an effort to do so. Unfortunately, they fall prey to inner fears, pride, inhibitions, stresses, self-defeat, and to a host of other inner weaknesses which, in effect, nullify their ability to heal. These people will never be able to self heal or group heal simply because they are chained down by earthly beliefs and habits. Most people on your earth plane find it more expedient to visit their doctor(s) whenever stresses or sicknesses confront them, and, of course, they are fully free to do so. As you know, doctors and nurses have a great responsibility and duty to perform in serving earth and its peoples. Most doctors on your earth plane, however, are extremely skeptical about spiritual healers and their healings, simply because many practicing spiritual healers have not used their inner talents soundly and wisely. These would-be healers merely pretend to heal people when, in truth, they do not. Consequently, most doctors require absolute proof of a spiritual healing from those claiming to be healed in this manner. As you know, it only takes a handful of false spiritual healers on your earth plane to create doubts in the hearts and minds of true, soul-searching people. Most doctors and millions of people around your world will continue to doubt and reject all types of spiritual healings as long as charlatan healers continue to thrive and abound.

Eventually, those who choose to become doctors will be taught the natural processes of healing once universally accepted on your earth plane. Future doctors will be called healers and will not follow your present day medical procedures, which are so dependent upon commonplace operative procedures for temporal or permanent healings or upon chemical drugs for temporal or permanent healings. This fact may sound regressive to some people on your earth plane today, but, in truth, the changes yet to come will be far more advanced and far more progressive than can be imagined! There are more and more people on your planet today who already attest that self healings, group healings, and herbal and plant healings are the way to a more enriched, holistic world. These people are ahead of their time and are in touch with the future! Nonetheless, all doctors and patients, all spiritual healers, and all natural healers on your planet should understand this one vital truth: God is and God will continue to be the ultimate Healer of all things. People can heal and cure themselves, or people may be healed and cured by someone else, but it is God who does the actual healing and curing.

Oscar, what basic procedures should be taken by a person attempting self healing or group healings?

Manuana, people cannot self heal or group heal unless they are tuned in to the healing forces or energies within their soul. The hands must be hot, and the person must have a sincere desire to heal, as well. In the case of an active spiritual healing, commonly known as the direct laying on of hands, whether upon self or upon another individual, a person must be in harmony with God, with self, with all life, and should implicitly believe in miracles. A disbelieving mind will not bring about positive results nor will harbored fears and pride. In the case of an absence healing created through meditation and prayer, a person must also be in league with God, with self, with all life, and should implicitly believe in miracles. Self-doubts, fears, and pride will not produce positive results in this type of healing either.

When you wish to do an active healing or an absence healing, you should close your eyes and commence to visualize yourself entering God's Clinic of Miracles. Upon entering, you should visualize yourself kneeling down in front of God's Holy Light and, within the silence and peace of your mind, you should commence to make a request or two for whomever you wish to help, heal, and cure. Always visualize His Holy Light, and silently commence to say this prayer:

> Oh Holy Father, I am your child; I am your seed. I humbly come to You for help, guidance, relief, and for a miraculous cure from the Glorious Bosom of Your Heart. Save (mention name) from the hardships of earthly strife and sickness now, and make (mention name) healthy now and productive now. Oh Holy Father, into your Loving Hands use me now! I beseech You, Father, please heal (mention name).

Keep repeating this plea until the vast reservoir of healing energy from your inner being is drained. The healing processes for an active healing may take an instant or two, or may take one-half hour earth time; the healing processes for an absence healing may also take an instant or two, or may take one hour earth time. If, for some reason, a healing does not take place at first, then you can be certain that the inner harmony in self or in whomever you wish to heal is not in total harmony with God. Some people try to self heal too prematurely or group heal too prematurely, without results, simply because their total attunement to God is lacking! Always remember that it is God who heals and cures, not the healer or the patient! And, if a series of many attempted spiritual healings fails, or all medical avenues of healing fail, then it may not be from one's lack of faith or trust in God, but may be God's Way of saying, "No, this healing will not be granted." There are daily occasions when He must say "No" to some requested healings, for a variety of reasons. He does this when He knows the request was untimely but will be granted in due time, or else when the soul of a patient is assigned by Him to leave planet Earth for a more enriched, Eternal Heavenly Life.

Will spiritual healing and natural healing remain alternatives to medical science, eventually play a greater role as a supplement to

*medical science, or will they completely replace medical science in
time to come?*

You will not see many attitudinal changes from the medical sciences regarding spiritual healers or natural healers in the
remaining years of the twentieth century, Manuana. However, it is during the beginning years of the twenty-first
century that quantum changes around your world will transpire. The prophecies of old must be fulfilled so that the
prophecies of a new and better earth can be fulfilled. And the
medical profession is no exception to this rule—for it too must
change drastically and spiritually when its "time and hour"
arrives. It is regrettable, however, that the science of medicine
in most countries of earth to date has failed to adopt spiritual
healing and its vast ancient philosophies and natural healing
and its vast ancient philosophies as supplements to their basic
medical teachings and practice. Had they done so, they would
then have been in league with the twenty-first century, now
fast approaching. This is not to imply that the medical profession on earth is not worthy or needed as it exists now—for it is
needed and wanted—but all three methods of healing could
have harmonized as an outstanding team to combat all the
incurable diseases still lingering on your planet Earth today.

There is not a disease on your planet that cannot be cured,
yet it simply cannot rest with one profession alone to try to
bring about all cures for all diseases known to man. Where
there is a disease, there is a virus; these elusive viruses have
created the mysterious stumbling blocks to actual cures. When
there is no hope for a patient at a hospital, a reputable spiritual
healer or a group of spiritual healers should be summoned to
try to cure this patient, or perhaps a cure might emanate from
a natural healer who has already created a simple herbal or
plant remedy for this patient's disease. With God, all types of
cures are possible! There should have been a worldwide team
network of spiritual healers, natural healers, and medical
healers created many years ago to assist mankind on earth;
unfortunately, this did not transpire. The medical system has

its own distinct "power camp," theories, and training, and will remain aloof from the other two needed, God-given healing groups until the twenty-first century. Then, a vast system of integrated spiritual changes will suddenly take place on planet Earth, and miraculous cures and remedies for all diseases will be forthcoming—and these diseases will be eradicated for all time.

There are many "miracle places" on earth one can visit to be spiritually, mentally, or physically healed. World-renowned places such as Our Lady of Lourdes in Lourdes, France; Our Lady of Fatima in Fatima, Portugal; Our Lady of Guadeloupe in Villa Madero, Mexico City; St. Mary's Church in Zeitoun, Egypt; and Our Lady of Knock in Knock, Ireland, are just a few of the places where many people have experienced miraculous healings. Why do these places not effect one hundred percent cures one hundred percent of the time? What, in essence, brings about an actual cure in these Holy places?

Your vast world is one Holy place of cures and miracles, Manuana, but in order to be cured, a person must have the inner faith to believe in God's Healing Ways and Miracles. Many people go to miracle shrines and places throughout your world to be cured of some disease, or to be cured of some infirmity, and, as you already know, a great number of people are miraculously saved and healed. These miracle places are God's Way of showing His Love to all His Children on earth! The Virgin Mary's appearances in a vast number of miracle places is to further advise mankind to love and respect God, the Creator of all Life, and to love and respect Jesus, His Son, and to pray earnestly for all sinners to change and to pray earnestly for world peace. Many people have heeded Her Holy Pleas, yet many have ignored Her Holy Pleas! Can you imagine how many times during a day your world uses God's Name, Jesus's Name, and the Virgin Mary's Name in vain? Can you imagine the patience and love God shows His Children on earth in spite of the many wrong things His Children persistently say and do against Him, His Son, and the Virgin

Mary? It is such a travesty and a shame, Manuana, that so many people on your earth plane utterly fail to see the vital importance of the Holy Virgin Mary's visitations. Yet, humbly, where She appears, many blessings and miracles are performed instantly and continue to be performed many years thereafter. Such Love and Help from God's Holy Emissary is living proof that God is Loving and Forgiving, that Jesus is Loving and Forgiving, and that the Holy Virgin Mary is Loving and Forgiving. Nevertheless, God does require more respect and appreciation from All His Children—not just from some of His Children.

What actually happens in these miracle places is that a host of Angel Masters and Angel Healers are left behind on site to heal those who humbly believe in the Mighty Miracles of God! (Any doubters who refute this truth may take their camera, with an infrared film, and may, on occasion, film these Angel Masters and Angel Healers at work. Any doubters who refute this truth may also use a high frequency parabolic microphone with a recorder, and may, on occasion, hear a chatter-type conversation of these Angel Masters and Angel Healers busily at work.) Even some people who half-believed in prayer, in miracles, and in God have been miraculously cured, simply because their half-beliefs soon became total beliefs in God, in prayer, and in miracles.

However, not everyone is cured in these Holy Places. Those who are cured can humbly be considered a true testimonial to God's Truth and Love; those who are not cured should still be grateful for God's Truth and Love. Sometimes people are not cured in these miracle places simply because their faith in self and in God is being tested and tried, and if they fail to comply, then no healing takes place—at least, not for the moment. But this is not to imply that a miraculous healing cannot or will not take place for these same people after they alter their negative thoughts and weaknesses in faith. A person should not give up simply because a healing was not or is not forthcoming. Sometimes a person must return several times or many times to a miracle shrine before an actual cure takes place. God Loves all His Children, and He Desires all His

Children to be healthy, but from time to time, He does test them before He rewards them! Giving up is tantamount to having little or no faith in self or in God.

Also note that a great number of cures have taken place around your world for people right in their own homes. These people simply prayed in front of a holy picture, a holy shrine, or a holy cross—only to realize shortly thereafter that they were cured! God is everywhere, and His Miraculous Cures are everywhere—all one has to do is believe Him, love Him, and trust Him. He will do the rest!

11

Phenomena

Oscar, will you explain and elaborate upon the following: stigmata, bleeding or weeping religious statues and pictures, astral projection, bilocation, poltergeist, automatic handwriting, psychic photography, prophetic dreaming, psychometry, telekinesis, premonitions, apports, levitation, and phone calls from the dead? Also, will you elaborate upon the Bermuda Triangle, the sasquatch or yeti, and, lastly, upon the Loch Ness monster?

STIGMATA

MANUANA, a stigmatist is an empath. This type of individual is born to serve his fellowman in a spiritual manner such as in a religious, prophetic, and healing manner. He is blessed this way to show earth the actual crucified wounds inflicted upon Jesus, the Messiah, many centuries past. So often people on your earth plane claim that a picture speaks a thousand words. Well, Manuana, the stigmatist is a living picture with Holy Proofs! Some stigmatists may have crucifixion wounds on their head, hands, feet, and sides such as Jesus experienced on the cross, or they may have a distinct crucifixion wound on their head alone, their hands alone, their feet alone, or, lastly, within their sides alone. Some stigmatists may also have stigmata signs or symbols on their head, hands, and feet which can alter from time to time. These stigmata signs or symbols are actual messages to earth from the Celestials of Light who emanate from distant universes. These messages are true, sincere signs that life abounds beyond planet Earth and that man is not unique to Earth alone. These Celestial message signs and symbols are further proofs that stigmatists are In His Service and that they must share their unique Heavenly gift messages with the world.

Stigmatists are not psychologically or religiously unbalanced in any manner as some people or some investigators on your earth plane might profess. No. They are deeply religious, both consciously and subconsciously, and tend to be unique and quite apart from your ordinary, average earthly citizen. Some are endowed with great insights and intelligence; some are endowed with average to simple intelligence and insights. Nevertheless, their wounds, signs, or symbols are all saintly gifts from God which they must share with their fellowman. Bear in mind, as well, that stigmatists are not born with these wounds, signs, or symbols. They receive these gifts as they grow and mature in life. Their empathic heart, mind, and soul are so attuned to God, to Jesus, and to life itself that when they least expect it, these wounds, signs, or symbols come upon them with miraculous swiftness, pain, and great inner joy. Their wounds, signs, or symbols are now permanent and will appear and reappear at random, or may appear and reappear on special holy occasions. These wounds, signs, and symbols are impressed upon them with an intense, radiated Light by Angel Masters from Heaven so assigned by God to do so!

BLEEDING OR WEEPING
RELIGIOUS STATUES AND PICTURES

Manuana, there are more bleeding statues and weeping pictures on your earth plane today than at any time in its entire history. Why? This is just another miraculous sign from God to teach and to advise His Children to pray, to change, and to believe in His Miraculous Ways. Sadly, though, many people on your earth plane still fail to recognize this Vital Message of Truth and continue in their wayward ways and habits! The twenty-first century is now fast approaching, and He wants His Children on earth to believe in Him and to serve Him—

not Satan and his demon helpers! The prophecies of old are fast approaching too, and with the traumatic changes yet to come, He earnestly desires all sinners of earth to peacefully change their negative beliefs, ways, and habits into positive beliefs, ways, and habits through prayer and solid actions. Those who listen to this Truth will prosper; those who fail to heed this Truth will sadly falter and fall.

Manuana, before a holy statue or picture commences to bleed or weep, there is an accumulative amount of prayer and earnest wishes surrounding it. One person may be praying and concentrating on the holy statue or picture at home or in church, or a group of people may be praying and concentrating on the holy statue or picture at home or in church. What is important is that the cumulation of many earnest prayers and many earnest wishes over a period of time invisibly surrounds the statue or picture like an unseen halo or holy mist. When these prayers and wishes reach a certain earthly spiritual zenith, or spiritual high frequency peak, God then assigns a Master Angel from Heaven to spill martyred blood and martyred tears or both onto the holy statue or holy picture. The blood and tears can flow periodically, or at times incessantly, and appear to come from nowhere—yet, miraculously, they are infused through radiated Sound and Light onto the holy statue or picture!

ASTRAL PROJECTION

All people on your earth plane astral wander or project on occasion while sleeping, but, unfortunately, only a small number of people are aware of this truth. Most people can only recall sleeping at night and waking up in the morning. They have no recollection of wandering out of their bodies at all. The true psychics, mediums, or mystics are certainly aware of their out-of-body travel and so are other true seekers attuned to this reality in life. Also note that some people especially attuned to their higher consciousness can, at will, astral travel when they are awake or half-awake. Astral travel can take place anytime during a heavy sleep state and lasts for only three minutes earth time. In the astral, this three-minute period appears like three hours! When the three minutes are up, the individual in the astral must instinctively return back to his body, otherwise a sleep death may occur. This type of death is not common, for most sleep deaths on your earth plane have other causes and reasons. Everything seen within the astral appears to have a white-blue light around it.

Now, a person may decide to talk to a friend or two, or may meet a stranger or two while journeying in the astral; may decide to visit a hospital or two in order to instill positive thoughts in those who are very sickly, depressed, or despondent; may decide to astral travel to far away places in order to instill positive thoughts and encouragements in less fortunate peoples of earth; or may simply decide to "astral visit" some area on earth in order to analyze this particular area before actually visiting it. Now assume, Manuana, that an individual met a stranger in the astral. Upon waking, everything is forgotten—but within a week or two, the individual surprisingly does meet this stranger! They seem to recognize one another and claim to have met before, but both parties simply cannot remember when or where. This form of "déjà vu" is most prevalent throughout your world! Now, assume further that an individual decided to astral visit some unfamiliar distant city or country which must actually be visited physically within the next month or so. The astral visit shows peace and harmony. Well, upon waking, everything is forgotten, but when this individual journeys to this distant city or country physically, almost everything in sight appears totally familiar! This individual seems to vaguely recall being in this distant city or country before but simply cannot remember when or how. This form of déjà vu is most prevalent throughout your world as well! Now, if the astral visit to some chosen location happened to reveal discontent, disharmony, or sadness, then within a day or two or more this individual may commence to have second thoughts about making this journey physically. The trip may be entirely cancelled because of some inner, unexplained feelings to do so; or the individual may ignore an inner feeling not to go, only to later find the visit upsetting and disappointing; or, lastly, the individual may ignore an inner feeling not to go and consequently dies in a tragic accident en route or dies at the destination point. Many inner warnings may come to a person on your earth plane in a variety of ways, but the two most prevalent ones are through astral warnings and through dream forewarnings.

A person who astral wanders during a wake state or semi-wake state is, of course, in a far better position to remember everything seen or heard. The time duration is three minutes which, again, appears like three hours, and most everything one sees or touches has a white-blue light around it. This mode of travel is instantaneous. Those gifted in this area merely step out of their body, think about a person, place, or thing, and before they know it, they are there! When the three minutes are up, they instinctively return to the physical body; failing to do so could result in one's untimely demise. This type of death is most uncommon on your earth plane as most people adhere to their instinctive time limit both safely and wisely!

BILOCATION

In extremely ancient times, people knew more about "dimensional travel" than people do today! Most cases of bilocation on your earth plane today may be attributed to the Celestials of Light within their "flying cars" who actually "beam" an individual, a vehicle, or something else from one location to another. Past saints, yogis, and other spiritually oriented individuals who were attuned to God were also tuned in to these Celestials of Light. Although the vast majority of these saintly beings on earth were not aware of this Celestial attunement, nonetheless, it was so and still continues to be so. It is these Celestials of Light who, frequently or infrequently, assisted saintly beings to bilocate, trilocate, or to travel to a multitude of places at one time. The methods employed by these Celestials of Light was to simply employ one beam of light, two beams of light, or three beams of "light travel" upon an individual—and lo and behold, one, two, three, or more places could be visited simultaneously. Sometimes, a Celestial of Light would join a saintly being or two while bilocation or trilocation was taking place. These Celestials of Light know of everyone on planet Earth now and from time immemorial and continue to assist saintly and other worthy beings today in the same frequency and manner as they did many centuries ago. These Celestials of Light may be considered the guardians of Earth. They are in league with God and should not, in any manner, be considered evil or dangerous. They are more loving and more caring than Earth can possibly visualize! Some of these Celestials of Light assigned to Earth hover above Earth in space, land on Earth, and have, on occasion, taken a person or two on board their flying cars for evaluation purposes. This should not be considered traumatic or frightening to anyone, for in the entire process of "colonization," it is their Universal Task to see that Earth people learn, prosper, and ultimately strive for peace. When man on Earth eventually becomes as the "gods" of old, he, too, will colonize other planets, and he, too, will periodically check upon his fold. This is precisely what some of these Celestials of Light have been assigned to do. Earth and its people are still infants compared to the light-year knowledge and wisdom these Celestials of Light possess! In time, these Celestials of Light will share many universal secrets with the meek who will yet inherit Earth!

Now, Manuana, the same method of light travel has occurred with some ordinary citizens on Earth and with some vehicles and their occupants on Earth. These occurrences today are attributed to unidentified flying objects and their beings. This is absolutely true. A single beam of light is emitted from their "flying car." This beam of light, which is highly energized and magnetized, simply falls upon an individual, a vehicle, or another object, and, hence, these are carried instantly from one location to another. Again, this process of "beaming" may appear frightening to some people, but it truly is not meant to traumatize in any manner! Earth is not being invaded by outer space creatures but is being monitored by these Celestials of Light who are, and who will continue to be, guardians of earth. When the King of Light returns to earth, their presence will then be more fully understood and appreciated!

Manuana, there is a mighty rare situation, however, when an individual actually does bilocate without any help or assistance from the Celestials of Light. How can an individual possibly bilocate without being assisted? Well, first of all, a person so attuned to this type of bilocation is somewhat of a daydreamer and is very determined. This person possesses a great amount of psychic ability, but does not know how to use it properly, or merely possesses a small amount of confused psychic ability. Before the actual bilocation takes place, a person suddenly becomes mentally, physically, and psychically disoriented. The person is suddenly chilled and senses some type of invisible entrapment is taking place but has no explanation for what is happening. What happens at this precise moment might be considered a freak of nature, or a freak of gravity, yet neither explanation is applicable. What actually happens here is that an "invisible whirlwind" from a dimension near earth crosses over into the physical dimension of earth through a space gap and instantly hovers over an individual receptive to its magnetic energy force field. This is not to imply that this so-called whirlwind is endowed with some type of intelligence, for this is simply not the case. Nor is this to imply that the individual involved has conjured this dimensional whirlwind in some manner, for this is not the case either. The mental psyche, electrical magnetism, and energy of this individual has by sheer coincidence locked itself into this dimensional whirlwind's magnetic energy force field. One could almost suggest that this strange dimensional whirlwind is similar to a tornado being phenomenally attracted to a trailer park! This hovering dimensional whirlwind, now attracted to this individual, silently swirls above his body. The individual now becomes totally disoriented. The whirlwind falls directly over him, totally encasing and transfixing him within the center core of its dimensional, invisible force field. Then instantly, he is carried away to an open field, highway, street, or some other point a mere mile or two away from the original location. No purpose has really been served in this type of bilocation other than to create some type of trauma within the individual's mind! This invisible whirlwind has now attracted itself to this person, and may, on another occasion, repeat the performance. The individual involved must commence to think and behave more positively and rationally, otherwise this dimensional attraction can persist for a year or two thereafter. Eventually, the attraction dissipates, the dimensional whirlwind disappears, and the body travel ceases to take place.

This truth should sound no more different and be no more unique than that of a physical being or some other solid object crossing over into the "invisible dimension" existing near earth. The frequency of people, ships, birds, animals, and so forth crossing over into this existing invisible dimension through earth's open doors and space gaps is far more prevalent than this rare type of whirlwind bilocation.

POLTERGEIST

People who are extremely stubborn, full of hate, spiteful, frustrated, and impatient can attract a poltergeist to themselves. Their confined anxieties are totally negative in nature. They often feel left out of some situation, or they feel that they are not needed or wanted for some real or imagined reasons. Puberty frustration, sexual frustration, middle age frustration, and old age frustration are often targets for poltergeist activities. The process of "negativity" within these individuals' mind can last for several or many years before their inner anxieties attract something unexpected, beyond their earthly power to perceive or handle.

Now, Manuana, when the actual poltergeist possession takes place, this is what transpires. An earthbound mischievous animal (normally a monkey), an earthbound soul (a ghost), or, lastly, a demon soul (one of Satan's assistants) enters the subconscious mind of a negative-minded individual. It is so tempted—it simply cannot resist! There it exists, and there it commences to possess and to create all types of havoc for that individual. When the earthbound or hellbound soul enters the subconscious mind of an individual, it can remain within this mind at its leisure, or it can walk out of this mind at its leisure, but it cannot escape! (To touch and tempt the subconscious mind of an individual is one matter, but to actually enter the subconscious mind of an individual is a serious infraction—a universally taboo intrusion. The subconscious mind of an individual should not be considered a sanctuary for an entity, no matter how tempting or alluring it may appear to be.) Now trapped, it desperately demands to be released! So in order to bring attention to this fact, the earthbound or hellbound soul commences to cause trouble, such as throwing chairs around, starting fires here and there, pulling the hair of or bruising the body of the individual who harbors it, and so forth. This soul utilizes its negative or mischievous invisible powers through solid matter quite easily and effectively. It uses its mind and body over solid matter through the powerful subconscious mind of an earthly individual. The mysterious subconscious mind is actually the channel or instrument it uses in order to gain attention.

In many respects, Manuana, the earthbound or hellbound soul is using its power and the power of the subconscious mind of an individual to effect a powerful form of telekinesis. And, of course, it does this—both day and night if necessary. It means business; it wants to be liberated quickly! It tries to plead its case in many ways, but unfortunately, those who are subjected to this type of possession simply do not know what is happening. They are too afraid, too mystified by the unusual occurrences taking place. They somehow feel that they are inwardly to blame, yet they cannot explain how or why. This activity will persist until help arrives or until some practical explanation on the subject of poltergeist is given to them. The earthbound or hellbound soul will be freed when an exorcist is called or when the individual involved commences to think and act more positively in life.

AUTOMATIC WRITING

All true mediums are capable of automatic writing, or prophetic writing as some may call it. Both the medium's writing hand and his chief guide's writing hand become as one when this phenomenon takes place. The chief guide overshadows a protégé's hand and then commences to write. Before the writings occur, however, a medium should have a positive mind, should avoid concentrating on the writings, drawings, or symbols, and should hold a pen gently above the paper until the actual writing commences. It would be an excellent testing suggestion for the medium to be reading a book in one hand while the other hand is being guided and controlled. At first, many scribblings will ensue until the attunement of hands is reached. When this attunement is reached, practical sentences and prophetic sentences commence to follow and flow. True mediums understand this very simple beginning to automatic writings better than anyone else. In time and with practice, the prophetic sentences and possible sketches and symbols become more startling and much more profound! Automatic handwriting is just one of many gifts true mediums develop over a period of time. This gift, Manuana, should not be taken lightly, for it is there to serve and teach, not to entertain.

PSYCHIC PHOTOGRAPHY

Those gifted with a "psychic thumb" are more likely to take successful psychic pictures than anyone else. Unfortunately, there are not too many people on your earth plane gifted in this manner. Those who are have an ample opportunity to reveal their pictures to those who doubt or to those who seek proof that life exists beyond the five senses. Let me make this notably clear, Manuana, that when an individual (with or without a psychic thumb) takes a psychic picture, it is not because the camera, film, location, or situation is unique or different. However, there are those rare exceptions when an infrared film may help in certain locations, such as at miracle places where some higher beings from Heaven simply cannot appear on ordinary film. Psychic pictures may be taken anywhere on earth and with any type of camera and film, providing permission is granted from this side of life for such phenomena to appear on a picture. Not everyone is granted this permission, no matter how hard one tries! If everyone was granted this permission, then there would be more psychic pictures than natural pictures on your earth plane, and this, of course, is simply not the case. A person may try to take hundreds of pictures of a supposed haunting of a house, castle, or graveyard, yet produce nothing phenomenal at all, while another person may casually come along and photograph the same area with phenomenal results! Why? Simply because the latter person was granted permission from this side of life, though not aware of this unique permission until the picture is emitted from the camera or until the film is developed. It is that factual and that simple!

PROPHETIC DREAMING

Any person who has a clear-visioned, reoccurring dream once a day for a week or two may consider this type of dream to be prophetic. The dream may pertain to a birth, a life-death situation, tragedy, death itself; or it may pertain to some other matter involving the dreamer personally, a family member, friend, acquaintance; or it may pertain to some catastrophic event about to happen. A prophetic dream may be a "blessing in disguise" to a dreamer, or it may be a warning that should be heeded at all times. This type of dream does not just happen by chance. It emanates from the soul of an individual into his subconscious dream. The soul, of course, is directly connected to God, and in His Mysterious Ways, He is attempting to reveal something vitally important to the dreamer. When forewarnings are clearly seen and forecasted within a dream of this nature, heed them!

Unfortunately, many people do not act upon their dream warning signs, only to later regret their indifference. Many tragedies and premature deaths could have been averted on your earth plane, Manuana, had more people heeded their God-given prophetic dreams!

PSYCHOMETRY

Some psychics are more gifted in psychometry than others. When they hold or touch an object, they immediately see a vision or two pertaining to the item they are holding. Their psychic, subconscious mind actually taps the source, the event, or anything else pertaining to the object they are holding and immediately reveals the impressioned truth still lingering on it. Some psychics are more talented in detective work than others, as many assist law enforcement agencies with their specialized gifts of psychometry and other similar psychic endowments.

TELEKINESIS

Very few people on your earth plane can actually perform telekinesis; when they do, it is very simple and limited. They may move a nail, a glass, or a pencil across a small table with their conscious and subconscious mind, or they may perform some other small or insignificant feat in this area of "mind over matter." But that is the summation of telekinesis on earth for the moment, Manuana. The ability to actually move objects with the mind cannot be performed on a large scale by any earth person simply because the earth-brain is not pro-grammed to be totally functional at this time. Only a small percentage of the earth-brain is presently functional. How-ever, there will come a time when a new generation will be born to earth. When this transpires, their earth-brain will be totally functional; they will become as the gods of old, and telekinesis will be among the many psychic gifts they will use humbly and wisely! The practice of telekinesis is constantly being utilized by higher beings on billions of habitable star systems now, Manuana, but earth must await its growth and its hour before this gift is universally bestowed upon its peoples.

PREMONITIONS

Precognizant forewarnings can be received by anyone on your earth plane, for everyone has this innate ability! When a sudden warning flashes into the conscious mind from your subconscious mind or appears as a sudden vision in front of you, be aware that something is terribly wrong! The life you save could be your own or that of another person. Or perhaps some sudden distressful news of a loved one is soon forthcoming. Whatever your mind reveals to you in these serious matters, or whatever you happen to see in a sudden vision, tread lightly and do your utmost to be cautious. It is during this sudden, stressful time, Manuana, that a person should commence to pray earnestly for the well-being of self and for the well-being of someone else possibly connected with the premonition.

Note that a premonition is similar to a prophetic dream except that its forewarning is only given once or twice during one's awake state. Again, premature deaths and tragedies might have been avoided if more people had heeded their premonitions cautiously and wisely!

APPORTS

Very few people on your earth plane can actually *will* objects, trinkets, or treasure from "nowhere," yet some physical mediums have this ability, some yogis have this ability, and some mystics have this ability, from birth. The mere handful of people who can perform this unusual feat, Manuana, have the unique ability to teleport objects, trinkets, or treasures from one location to another within their own physical dimension; can teleport them within their own physical dimension to themselves; or can, at times, teleport them to themselves from a dimension closest to your planet Earth. (Often, these people attract treasures or artifacts from ships or other vehicles which crossed over to the fourth dimension.) They are ahead of their time in these matters, but, then again, there is a sound, valid reason for their unique talents. What actually transpires here, Manuana, is that this handful of people on your earth plane is blessed with two subconscious minds from birth—not one! One subconscious mind is more than powerful, but being blessed with two powerful subconscious minds along with a hearty conscious mind can and does produce those startling, mystifying objects from thin air called apports. These people are simply doubly blessed in that they can demonstrate man's futuristic abilities to those who disbelieve in futuristic truths or to those who humbly seek solid futuristic truths.

LEVITATION

Manuana, most people on your earth plane have the inner capabilities of levitating providing they seek and they find the Christ Light within them. Some true mediums, mystics, yogis, and saints could levitate after meditation, praying, and fasting. They all sincerely wanted to reach the Christ Light within themselves—and they did! Nothing is impossible to anyone on your earth plane providing he believes in God and in self, and makes the necessary efforts to achieve his ultimate goals! When Jesus, the King of Light, was on your earth plane, Manuana, He not only walked on land, but He also walked on air and water! He conquered all the elements known to man simply because He had no doubts about His ability to do so, and His Faith was in total harmony with these elements. A person must completely let go of all inner fears, hatreds, and inhibitions before the process of levitation can take place. A person must, in truth, become pure in mind, heart, and soul before levitation becomes a reality. Levitation itself is no more than rising above a force of air below one's body and feet. And, Manuana, the secret to rising above this natural force of air simply involves absolute Faith in all things.

The door to levitation is open to anyone willing to seek and to find these truths, for, indeed, man can learn to walk on air and water, but he must first rise above himself and his earthly fears and weaknesses.

PHONE CALLS FROM THE DEAD

These telephone call connections originate from some of the Celestials of Light near earth. They simply direct their "communication beam" at a soul now in the first Learning Mansion. This soul then talks into the beam to a loved one on your earth plane. This communication is genuine and sincere and should be considered loving—not frightening. When a person on your earth plane receives this type of telephone call, a sudden trancelike state is experienced. Why? Well, for a moment or two, a person receiving this call becomes like a true medium on your earth plane, Manuana. As you know, mediums can communicate to this side of life through trance states, through prophetic hearing, and other ways, but many people on earth are not inclined to accept this truth unless they experience something similar. When they actually receive a telephone call from a deceased loved one, they are totally dumbfounded at first—and then become totally ecstatic once they realize what happened!

Manuana, the Celestials of Light have been assigned to make these vast telephone connections to earth as a sign for earth people to believe beyond their five senses of doubts and wonder. *Life does exist after death, and life does exist in outer space!* How can they possibly convince earth to accept this Universal Reality? These genuine "beam communication" calls will persist until more and more people on your earth plane are genuinely convinced of this truth.

BERMUDA TRIANGLE

All planets have "time dimensions." Earth, of course, is no exception to this rule. Planets that are suitable for life have an even number of time dimensions; planets that are not suitable for life (planets that are similar to your moon for exploration and mining purposes, and planets that are completely poisonous and taboo for man's existence) have only one time dimension. The time dimension on these exploratory planets and planets unsuitable for sustaining life is unwholesome. In your solar system, there are only two other planets that have an even number of time doors—Venus and Mars. These two planets will eventually be colonized by Earth and will have all the exact, life-sustaining genetic elements Earth has. The Celestials of Light will eventually teach man on Earth the simple, yet complex process of igniting and seeding a planet to life. Both Venus and Mars will be known as man's first quantum steps towards colonization, for man, too, must become as the gods of old. And he will! Your moon has no time dimensions at all, for it is inactive and hollow, whereas your active sun has one enormous time dimension, as all stars do. Eventually, when your sun dies, its body mass will fuse with its one invisible time dimension to become a black hole or space hole. A black hole then becomes an enormous space tunnel. These space tunnels are frequently used by more highly developed beings throughout the multitude of universes in existence. Simply visualize the long metal tube attached to a vacuum cleaner, Manuana. When turned on, it quickly takes hold of an object and pulls it in. The same principle applies to a black hole. When these higher beings, with their "space cars or ships" enter one, they are in complete control of their vehicles within a black hole's powerful suction. Using a black hole saves time; it is a shortcut in travelling from one universe to another. Now, the Bermuda Triangle is just one of the many places on earth where a time door, a space gap, or an earth window just happens to open and close at random. A "time door" is like a gigantic invisible wall with an opening to it. This time door can shift from one location to another within the Bermuda Triangle as do similar time doors in other locations around your world. This shifting, Manuana, can be unpredictable! When a ship or airplane enters this first time dimension, commonly called the "fourth dimension" on your earth plane, it simply vanishes from sight. The airplane or ship has approximately one hour earth time to simply turn around quickly and go back from whence it came before the time door seals itself shut! Unfortunately, there is electrical static and a certain amount of mental confusion on board when an airplane or ship enters the first time dimension. Those in charge search for sound or practical guidances to their dilemma, but their instruments fail, and all communication with the outside world grows fainter and fainter until it is ultimately lost. They simply fail to realize that by turning around quickly and going back from whence they came, they will, once more, be back in their real world. Regretfully, the time door closes while they frantically search for practical reasons and answers to their dilemma. Consequently, they become locked in the first time dimension.

The first time dimension within the fourth dimension can be called the "past-present" time dimension. Upon entering it, a person still sees the sun, the moon, calm waters, a slow moving cloud or two, and perhaps a bewildered bird or two flying here and there. Everything appears natural and normal, except there are no buildings present and absolutely everything in sight is still, calm, and peaceful. The world here appears like a wilderness or like nature's finest hour, for it is very beautiful to behold. The weather remains constantly warm, pleasant, and summerlike throughout this entire "past-present" dimension. There are no seasons or great tempests here. The stream water is drinkable, and there are edible berries and wild apple trees scattered here and there. It is like stepping back into the sixteenth century on earth with no one there to greet you, to guide you, or to protect you. In many respects it may best be described as earth having closed each individual chapter to all its past centuries and stored them naturally within this "past-present" dimension. And this, of course, it does—except each century now stored away is devoid of people, places, and things long past from planet Earth. If a person chose to remain within this "past-present" time dimension, Manuana, death would inevitably follow. Lack of needed sustenance, loneliness, and boredom would be the ultimate reasons for death. Some chose this route, whereas some forged onward until they haphazardly reached the "second" time dimension.

The second time dimension on earth within your so-called fourth dimension can be called the "future-present" time dimension. Upon entry into this dimension, most everything appears relatively calm, still, warm, and pleasant to behold except for those sudden electrical "odd" swirls of wind seen now and again. The surroundings may be different, but everything is of earth and still appears to be one vast wilderness with no one there to greet you, to guide you, or to protect you. The only inner difference one commences to experience within this second time dimension, Manuana, is a strange, higher frequency of thought and of mind. What actually happens is that the "genetic programmed brain" of a person commences to open up a bit more within this dimension. One suddenly begins to perceive life a bit more clearly, realizing, as well, that there is no possibility of ever returning back home to the so-called "real world." Now, scattered throughout this second dimension are small, human-sized "time doors" invisible to the naked eye. Once entrapped, an individual is suddenly locked into another time warp, disappears, becomes invisibly coma-tose in a web of molecular light and commences to make a "time journey" to another habitable planet or perhaps back to planet Earth. It is extremely rare for an individual to be brought back to planet Earth at a future date in this manner, yet this has happened to an individual or two in earth's past. Upon one's arrival to another habitable planet, or to planet Earth if this be the rare case, the time traveller materializes, wakes up, is slightly dazed, and senses that only a minute or two has passed by. Yet, in truth, one hundred to seven hundred earth years have elapsed with this time journey.

Manuana, this form of time travel may be considered extremely slow by the Celestials of Light or by other higher beings throughout the entire Cosmos. But, nonetheless, this slower type of time travel through a planetary dimension does exist. I should also bring to your attention that the Celestials of Light and other higher beings throughout the entire Cosmos actually have time machines to take them deep into the future if that is their need. The time lost to them, or the time lost on their planet while they make their journey both there and back, is extremely minimal. I should mention, as well, that the Celestials of Light and other higher beings make journeys into deep space without experiencing extreme time losses. They use mapped highways and byways in space and black holes, and, of course, their "flying cars and ships" are propelled by life's natural, inexpensive "magnetic-energy forces" existing every-where. The speeds they reach in their "flying cars and ships" are quantum light-years beyond earth's natural light and natu-ral sound! In time, man on earth will also build and fly these "flying cars and ships" and will explore a host of galaxies and universes beyond his home planet and will commence to uncover these many hidden truths.

SASQUATCH OR YETI

Manuana, the sasquatch and yeti are extremely distant cousins to the Neanderthal man who once inhabited Earth. The sasquatch and yeti are not of Earth but have been brought to your planet by the Celestials of Light for survival purposes. They are closely watched over by the Celestials of Light and will, one day, disappear again from your planet. It simply appears that your Earth planet is conducive to their particular needs for survival, and they have been temporarily placed there until their needs are fulfilled. These beings are not animals but are primitive beings from distant star systems. They are extremely intelligent and simply know that they cannot mix or mingle with earth beings. Their fur covering is protected by sulfur-smelling oils so as to shield them from preying animals and preying hunters. They are extremely tall, strong, fast, and elusive—and communicate to one another mentally and with their barks and howling sounds. Eventually, they will be taken off your planet by the Celestials of Light. When this happens, they will be taken to a new planetary system similar to Earth's where they will continue to flourish and prosper. Be aware, as well, that these beings can survive on habitable planets which would be extremely harsh, severe, and cold to man. They are excellent miners and naturalists!

THE LOCH NESS MONSTER

Manuana, there is a host of giant serpents and creatures that abide in Earth's deep lakes, seas, and oceans. The Loch Ness monster, an extremely distant relative to the prehistoric plesiosaur, is closely guarded and watched over by the Celestials of Light, as are the other creatures I speak about. They are all elusive, shy, and normally roam in deeper waters where man does not or cannot tread. The Loch Ness monster can be from forty to sixty feet long. It feeds on water plankton and the odd fish and upon other fine plant life growing above water or upon other fine plant life thriving in deep waters. Although they are big creatures, they are not big eaters! It is difficult for man to comprehend why he cannot manage to capture, tag, and catalogue a giant, prehistoric, reptilian creature like the Loch Ness monster and other such creatures when he has been so successful in recording the propagation and survival of such prehistoric creatures as the insect and the turtle! Herein lies a true mystery for man to unravel—ultimately, he will.

12

Organized Religion

Oscar, how did the Bible originate? Why is it that so many passages are interpreted in so many different ways? Why do certain parts of the Bible portray God as someone who "orders" His children to war in His name?

MANUANA, the Bible is an accumulation of ancient thoughts, hearsay, handed-down stories, and some God-given inspiration by ordinary people. These handed-down "thoughts" were later compiled and written down by some ancient evangelists who wished the world to gain by its teachings. You must remember that these accumulated thoughts and stories were written down over a century after Jesus departed from your earth plane. During Jesus's lifetime on earth, there was nothing written about Him. Biblical thoughts and handed-down stories were written down much later, and eventually these were accepted, long after His departure from earth. Many actual truths, however, were lost in the process of its writing, and many man-made additions and inspirations were eventually added to or deleted from the original ancient texts as centuries went by. Today, there are nearly nine hundred versions of the Bible around planet Earth.

One can interpret its writings and its teachings in many different ways—for in those days the writings had many man-made, symbolic, hidden meanings and some God-given revelations. It was then up to man to either decipher, accept, or reject its teachings as being the total Word of God, or for man to use common sense in weeding out some of those man-made stories within its texts and teachings. You must always bear this in mind: the Bible was written long after Jesus's departure from your earth plane, and many actual truths were totally lost to oblivion long before it was written. It would be the same principle as for someone on your earth plane today to write about some handed-down stories from a past century or two. Some truths might still be intact, some truths would be lost due to time factors, and lastly, some stories would merely be assumed or fabricated. Such are the writings of the Bible except for those God-given truths man must seek and find within its teachings. Nonetheless, one should not ignore God's Holy Rules from an ancient time, nor should one ignore the basic life of Jesus while He was on your earth plane, and, of course, one should not ignore the God-given ancient prophecies that belong to your present day and age. In reading the Bible, one should read it with an open mind, not with a closed mind, fanatical mind, overzealous mind, hateful mind, or with a totally disbelieving mind. God works in many ways, and the Bible should be considered as a book of recollections and impressions from ancient times to your present day and age, with some truths intact—some not. When the King of Light returns to your earth plane, Manuana, the Infallible Truths of God will be revealed to mankind so that, at last, man will commence to comprehend God's True Love and God's True Laws.

God does not command His Children to go to war in His Name, Manuana! One of His Holy Rules is not to murder, so why would He command His Children to go to war to kill? When His Son was born to your planet, His Son taught only peace, love, and harmony. God upholds His Son's Belief, for it is man who thrives on war and killing, not God, the Creator of All Life! This, again, is where common sense should prevail when reading Biblical stories and teachings. God does not wish to frighten His Children to Him; He wishes His Children to come unto Him in peace, in faithful worship, in great love, and with deep respect. If more people would commence to realize that God forgives them thousands of times during their lifetime, they would then simply understand that God truly Loves them from birth to death—to Eternity! God is not violent, obscene, uncaring, unloving, spiteful, revengeful, lustful, warlike, or anything else that might be considered evil! God is not evil—*God is total love!* He may be stern at times, but He is not sinful!

Man, however, can be attracted to evils by adhering to his own selfish, prideful ways or by adhering to Satan and his many legions of sinful helpers. Sadly, many people are actually afraid of God due to some misinterpretations, frightening stories, and inaccuracies contained within the Bible and due to their overall positive-negative religious teachings and upbringings. If more people would simply realize that God is Loving and Caring, and that He Wishes All His Children to live peacefully and abide faithfully with one another, there would be more harmony. However, it seems, Manuana, that many people of earth must pass on to this side of life before His Love can be visibly seen and ultimately accepted. In life, Manuana, a person should worship, love, and respect God; a person should love and respect Jesus and the Virgin Mary; and, just as importantly, a person should love and respect self and one's fellowman at all times. These five guidelines are true and will stand the test of time both now and forevermore!

Where are the Papacy and other religions on earth headed?

The papacy like all other religious states and orders on earth is headed towards the Truth, the Light, and the Love yet awaiting all planet Earth! As yet, Manuana, there is no one totally true religious church state on your planet. An individual alone who worships, loves, and respects God; an individual alone who loves and respects Jesus and the Virgin Mary; and, an individual alone who loves and respects self and all earth is in league with God's True Church! There is no other church that can be considered holy except the inner Holy Church of God that abides within every man, woman, and child. It is up to each responsive individual to seek and to ultimately find His Church within his own thoughts, actions, and deeds in life. Controlled teachings can bring about controlled thoughts which God does not want of His Children. He wants all His Children to be free to learn, to be free to express their views, to be loving, and to be caring towards all life that is and all life that will ever be. He wants all His Children to soar like eagles in positive thoughts and actions, so that their brief learning sojourn on earth can be vitally useful and invaluable to them on this Eternal side of life. However, man-made religious restrictions, secrets, and fallacies have shackled mankind for centuries, thus not allowing him to change or to be inspired by God except for those few saintly beings, both known and unknown, who intelligently tapped into God's Reservoir of Love within them.

When Jesus was on your earth plane, Manuana, He did not force anyone to accept His Truths, nor did He control anyone to accept His Truths. He freely spoke the Truth of God, and then it was entirely up to an individual to either accept or reject this Truth. Each religious church on your earth plane claims to possess ultimate truths; each can create bitter wars and indifferences with one another and consequently do. Sadly, many fail to teach that religion itself was always meant to be "a personal, liberated soul search for God in a positive way; a personal, liberated way of practicing life in a positive way" at all times, not just under the cloak of a church. Bear in mind, as well, Manuana, that when souls enter the first Learning Mansion on this side of life, it is not their earthly church or religion that will gain them entry. It is their individual, inner, positive beliefs and faith in God, and their individual, positive thoughts and actions fulfilled in life that will bid them enter.

What was Jesus's mission in life? Where was He during the "unknown" years of His life? What was and is the Virgin Mary's mission on earth?

Manuana, Jesus's mission was to teach mankind the way to God and to teach mankind the way to a truer understanding of life and of death. His arrival was prophesied years before His actual birth to Earth, as you and millions of others on your earth plane implicitly believe. He ultimately came, He ultimately taught man, and He ultimately conquered all elements known to man. He was and is the One Special Son of God—but remember that all peoples on your earth plane are also special sons and daughters of God. Jesus was and is infallible! He was and is the radiated pure Light of God; He was and is the Messiah to mankind; He was and is the ultimate Breath of Truth of God, His Father! To behold Jesus is to behold His Father, is to behold all Love that was and is, all Truth that was and is, and all Joys that will ever be! The pureness of His Soul is like seeing your sun a billion times brighter than it is or like seeing the pureness of life itself encased in one pure mind and one pure body. There are various pictures on your earth plane today that do resemble Jesus rather closely. He was taller than the average individual on your earth plane in those days. He was always extremely humble, caring, and loving towards everyone He met. As well, the inner knowledge He was endowed with at birth could be considered total genius, for His Mind was completely open and functional! He was totally mediumistic, for He saw many unseen truths, visions, and prophecies ordinary people could not see or behold. He knew His Life's Missions on earth. He carried them out, and He succeeded in all these measures!

The supposed "lost years" of Jesus were not lost at all, Manuana. They were simply not recorded or monitored by any reporters in those days. Where was Jesus during His growing up years? Simply put, Manuana, He was with and beside His earthly parents most of the time. Jesus could bilocate, trilocate, and wander to a multitude of places at once and at will. On many occasions, He did wander to many places around earth in this manner to see what planet Earth was all about. He also taught some peoples in various places on earth during His multiple visits. He also communicated with angels or space beings who revealed many Universal Truths to Him. He knew when His Time to teach on earth was ripe, He knew when His Teachings would be fulfilled, and He also knew of His assigned Mission and destiny to "rise above the cross of death" in life.

The Virgin Mary's mission an earth, Manuana, was to give birth to Jesus. The pureness of her soul was chosen by God to conceive His Holy Son on earth. And it did come to pass, and He was born in a small "cave" in Bethlehem. Such humble beginnings are God's Way to teach mankind to be humble! The pureness of the Virgin Mary's Light represents all true womanhood and motherhood in all the Universes for, indeed, Her love towards God, towards Her Son Jesus, and towards mankind was and is infinitely purer and brighter than a host of stars combined. There are various pictures and statues that do resemble Her on your earth plane, Manuana. She prays constantly for "earth's welfare," desires sinners to change and to believe in God, desires earth to glorify God, desires earth to respect Her Son's Wishes for Peace, and desires earth to pray against all known evils. Those who respect Her pleas will "gain" threefold; those who do not will be saddened in time to come. She is and will continue to be God's Holy Emissary to earth until prophecies of old are fulfilled and until Jesus, the Messiah, returns to earth and is glorified by earth as He is in Heaven!

13

Wisdom Left Behind

Oscar, will you explain and elaborate upon the following: the Great Pyramid of Cheops, the Sphinx, desert markings in Peru, the megaliths, Easter Island statues, the Dead Sea Scrolls, and the Zodiac.

THE GREAT PYRAMID OF CHEOPS

MANUANA, the great pyramid on earth was built by the Celestials of Light who came in remote millennia. This pyramid is far more ancient than presently speculated and recorded, and was built as a temporal base for communication purposes and for astronomical purposes. The actual building of this great pyramid and several others nearby was considered necessary and practical at the time. Had there been a mountain range in that specific location of Egypt, the pyramid buildings would not have been necessary. A mountain range would have sufficed for their immediate wants and needs, but this, of course, was not available. Hence, these pyramids were built! The Celestials of Light merely "beamed" their rays from their "space cars" above a distant quarry, cut blocks of stone with detailed precision, transported them to their chosen sites instantly, and in a short order of time, built this great pyramid along with several others nearby. What may appear majestic, awesome, and impossible to build by earth man today, would be considered microscopically simplistic by these Celestials of Light then. It was not built by slaves as was often postulated and believed by ancient peoples, or as is still believed by some scientists and some theorists on your earth plane today. (However, those smaller, poorly built, man-made pyramids left behind, "mere imitations," cannot compare to the Celestials-built pyramids.) Nor was this pyramid intended as a burial place for kings or queens in ancient times. The paintings and symbols within were done centuries later by man. Consider the great pyramid of Egypt and its surrounding areas as being one of earth's first temporary communication and observatory headquarters and one of earth's first temporary air bases built by the Celestials of Light. In time to come, man will discover many pyramids on other planetary systems that were built identically to that of earth's and surprisingly, built by the same people.

THE SPHINX

The ancient Sphinx was created by the Celestials of Light as a lasting memory or memento to earth and its future. This massive figure represents a third planet in a small solar system wherein man and animal must coexist. Also note that the Celestials of Light used the sphinx design as a crest on their space suits. This merely depicted their "colonizing" status throughout the Universes. Man will eventually discover other Sphinx figures on other planetary systems!

DESERT MARKINGS IN PERU

These bird, insect, and other ancient land drawings were created by the Celestials of Light with their "space car" beams. These drawings were created just as quickly as a child might draw a picture on a piece of paper! They served as a safe landing guide for their space vehicles and also served as a directional flying guide for their pilots. These markings can, as well, be found in other areas of earth serving the same purpose. Again, their knowledge and expertise in matters of space colonization, in matters of repairing earth after some cataclysmic event, and in matters of using air signs and symbols is light-years beyond earth's comprehension. Even today, man seeks the roots to his past, often believing that his ancient earth ancestors were far more knowledgeable and far more gifted than he is today. This, of course, is simply not the case! The vast mysteries of earth's past may be attributed to the many mysterious artifacts, monoliths, statues, strange writings, and so forth left behind by Celestials of Light who were and still are space colonizers, space engineers—and space cousins!

THE MEGALITHS

Again, Manuana, the mysterious megaliths such as Stonehenge were created by the Celestials of Light in ancient times. The construction was simple and fast. With their air vehicles, they transported these stones from a distance. Upon returning to the chosen spot, they made large holes in the ground with their air rays, and then plunged and sealed these stones in the earth from the air in a circular fashion. These megaliths were devised for astronomy purposes. Some theorists on your earth plane have already deduced this fact, and they are correct! However, these megaliths were not devised by man's early ancestors, for man's early ancestors were far more simple in their ways and were far more baffled by earth's megaliths and vast secrets than man is today.

EASTER ISLAND STATUES

These giant statues on Easter Island, as well as some others around earth, should give you some idea as to what some of the ancient Celestials of Light looked like. These impressive, distant-staring statues were all created by the space colonizers as a lasting memory or memento to earth and its future. Man often affirms that a picture speaks a thousand words—yet, what does a timeless statue tell man? There are many different types of ancient, mysterious statues around your earth plane today, Manuana. Some of these ancient statues resemble earth people—some do not! Let it be known now that a host of Celestials of Light do resemble earth people—others do not!

THE DEAD SEA SCROLLS

There are more "hidden" scrolls to be found near the Dead Sea, Manuana. These will be found in due time. The Dead Sea scrolls basically depicted a sect of people called the Essenes who lived near Jerusalem and the Dead Sea. This sect, however, was created centuries before Jesus's birth, after their initial encounter with the Celestials of Light. Their simple, secular way of life, their love of nature, and their limited understanding of God was, in many ways, similar to some Christian orders on your earth plane today. As Jesus was growing up (the "hidden" years), He met with them, He talked with them. However, they were not the ones to instill knowledge in Him—it was Jesus who instilled more knowledge in them! Jesus knew about His Father, about life, and about death—and He was willing and content to share His wealth of knowledge with these humble people, and this He did most admirably!

THE ZODIAC

The ancient science of astrology may be connected to ancient Babylonia because of their known limited knowledge about certain planets and star systems, but its first teachings from the Celestials of Light came to earth's ancient beings in the Middle East and Asia Minor. This science might very well express man's first attempts at astronomy, for it does represent the sun, the moon, the planets, and twelve constellations. The zodiac is like a time clock whose planetary systems above the horizon, or whose planetary systems below the horizon, have an influence upon one's life and character. This science can be phenomenally accurate—and is, to this very day and age, basically used to guide and assist people. Many people on your earth tend to frown upon or disbelieve in astrology. However, if they were given the opportunity to have a careful reading or chart prepared by a competent astrologer, they would be amazed at its accuracy.

Oscar, is there such a place as Shangri-La in Tibet?

In extremely ancient times, Manuana, there was a place deep within the Himalayan mountains of Tibet that could very well be considered a Shangri-La. It was futuristic in appearance, and one could say it had the many luxurious conveniences earth has today. This Shangri-La settlement was inhabited by the Celestials of Light or by "handsome space gods" as they were known to some in extreme antiquity. Their settlement, amidst three snow-capped mountains and lush fertile fields, was well hidden, was temporary, and could very well be considered a resting place or resort for them on earth. It would have been impossible for any earth being to locate this city then, simply because access to this unique, legendary place on earth was by air only. The city of Shangri-La does not exist on your planet any more; yet, sadly, man still yearns to find it.

Manuana, Tibet is a mystical place of beauty, for truly it is a land of mystery, phenomena, and great hidden wonders yet to be explored by man. The climate may not always be to one's liking, but the altitude is certainly conducive to one's psychic or mediumistic talents. The awareness of life simply becomes more acute within this ancient land created for mystics, poets, and prophets. It is here where a person's inner gifts and abilities can be fulfilled and satisfied, and where prayer and meditation become synonymous with life itself. Inner peace within this strange, alluring country can bring wisdom, as I once discovered many centuries ago.

Oscar, will you explain and elaborate upon the following: what is a fire-breathing dragon, and what destroyed the dinosaurs?

FIRE-BREATHING DRAGON

Manuana, there is no such creature as a fire-breathing dragon anywhere in all the universes, nor did such a creature ever exist on your earth plane! In ancient times, whenever people saw a radiated "space car" in the sky or on land, they would attribute this unknown thing to an imaginary fire-breathing dragon or to some other creature or symbol. In some respects the space car's speed, light, insignias, and overall appearance reminded ancient peoples of fast moving serpents, lizards, or some other creature or symbol. Whenever the space car moved across the sky in a zigzag manner, bouncing manner, or slow, descending manner, they would attribute this strange sight to an imaginary fire-breathing dragon or to some other creature or symbol. Or, whenever a space car landed, the radiated light around it would frighten observers here and there, and once more this unknown sight would be attributed to an imaginary, fire-breathing dragon or to some other creature or symbol. Many fictitious legends were born this way on earth, Manuana, simply because people in those days did not know any better.

DINOSAURS

The dinosaurs on planet Earth were destroyed by a sudden shift in the earth's inner structure. This cataclysmic event, which brought about continued massive earthquakes around planet Earth, changed the climate for a very brief period of time and dramatically brought about rampant, deadly poisons to these prehistoric creatures both on land and in water. Earth's entire inner web made a drastic, sudden shift, spewing out deadly gases throughout planet Earth. Hence, all these giant creatures were suddenly destroyed by the earthquakes and by the deadly gases. They quickly disappeared from Earth within a month's span as though they never existed! Plant life and smaller creatures were also destroyed throughout the Earth, but some survived this sudden, extremely brief period of extinction. However, it should also be known that before this sudden event transpired on Earth, many pairs of each species of ancient dinosaurs were stunned, gathered, and then transported to another star system for further breeding purposes. The dinosaurs were transported by the Celestials of Light in their massive cargo spaceships. They were placed on another planet quite similar to Earth and quite similar to Earth's prehistoric beginnings.

14

The Universe

Oscar, what is Earth's true Genesis?

EARTH'S TRUE GENESIS is like any other planet in all the universes. A planet is formed from a star's mixture of gases and debris. To sustain life, a planet must have two hidden dimensions to it, and Earth, of course, met those requirements. Venus and Mars, near Earth, are the best examples of what Earth looked like in its infancy, Manuana. When Earth was first "ignited" and "seeded" by the ancient Celestials of Light so assigned by God to do so, they had already colonized millions upon millions of other star systems. Their tasks were to instill life throughout the universes and to colonize life throughout the universes. To this very day, this process of spreading life is still taking place, by them and by others in league with God. Man on Earth will eventually do the same, so that his species, which abounds in other star systems, may continue to grow and flourish in his universe. Man on Earth will one day be as the "space gods" of old!

Now, when planet Earth was first "ignited" and "seeded," millions of years elapsed before other preparatory stages towards more advanced life were introduced to it. Each individual era on a planet must harmonize and must benefit a higher species of life yet assigned to come forth. When all signs were ripe and ready, and when all prehistoric eras served their ideal purposes on planet Earth, the ancient Celestials of Light planted some prehistoric, apelike beings there. These apelike beings were from another star system planet which was similar to Earth in those days. Hence, this "planting of life" became the first era of man's early beginnings and man's early survival on Earth.

After millions of years had elapsed, these apelike beings developed rather moderately and changed rather moderately, but nonetheless, they still served their purpose in the process of modern man's evolution. Again, when the time was ripe and ready, the genetic code in man was then introduced to planet Earth. After a cataclysmic event took place some 32,000 years ago, the Celestials of Light repaired Earth. This took 3,500 years. When this was accomplished, the Celestials of Light commenced to introduce their "procreative and genetic seeds" into the wombs of earthly female survivors in a breeding place called the Garden of Eden. This Garden of Eden was located in Asia Minor! Hence, after 16,000 years of careful genetic engineering, monitoring, and isolation, intelligent life was, at last, born to Earth. The simple, apelike beings simply ceased to exist, for they were now modern-like, intelligent beings! The different colored male and female species born on your planet were later assigned to different areas of Earth more conducive to their genetic makeup and structure. For example, the dark skinned species of man were to abide in torrid climates, the yellow skinned species of man were to abide in moderate to hot climates, and the white skinned species of man were to abide in warm, moderate, or cold climates. Hence, different species of intelligent man were placed throughout your planet to begin their first civilized cultures. At first, they were under the watchful eye and guidance of the Celestials of Light, then eventually they were left on their own for hundreds of years at a time so that they could find their own way in life. Yet, from time to time, the Celestials of Light would return, would settle on Earth again, would build lasting monuments, monoliths, and so forth, and would teach the different cultures new areas of learning, such as tool making, agriculture, mathematics, star systems, and so forth. Hence, Manuana, all known ancient cultures on your earth plane had their first direction and learning from the ancient creators known as the Celestials of Light. Man is a direct descendant from the stars, which he, too, will eventually seek, seed, and propagate.

Over the centuries there have been many wars on planet Earth, Oscar. Why did the Celestials of Light allow this?

Manuana, all civilizations on your planet must learn the rights from the wrongs along their progressive journeys and struggles in life. In the beginning, the Celestials of Light repeatedly counselled their "offspring" to live in peace and harmony. At first they did, but as time went by, and new offspring were born, many rebelled, and many did not heed their true heritage and beginnings. Then eventually, God gave His Holy Rules to Earth so that man could abide by these Holy Rules. Many listened, but many did not. God then gave His Son to Earth so that man would listen and cherish His Words! Many did cherish His Words, but many did not. So, even up to your present day and age, Manuana, man continues to overshadow God's Rules of peace and harmony for his own rules of peace and war! A third and final "Higher Intervention" will one day transpire on planet Earth, and it is *then* that the chaff will be separated from the wheat and that man, at last, will find his true, peaceful beginnings. The pure and the meek left behind will survive and will fulfill man's rightful destiny! Earth will eventually know total peace, as it, too, must find its rightful place in the Federation of Star Systems.

Oscar, are there other star systems with warlike people?

No, Manuana. All other star systems are peaceful and thrive in intergalactic harmony. If this were not true, your planet would have been annihilated centuries ago! Total peace, love, and understanding must abound on a planet before it can truly progress both inwardly and outwardly. Love, harmony, and understanding are all progressive ways in life; all evils are suppressive! The difficulty on planet Earth, Manuana, is that many people find it more expedient to do wrong to themselves and to others than to do good! Leaders in all walks of life who know better, should serve better, but they do not. Parents in all walks of life who know better, should guide better, but they do not. Children in all walks of life who know better, should learn to understand better, but they do not. "An eye for an eye and a tooth for a tooth" is not God's Way nor will this ever be His Way! Revenge, greed, and pride can lead a soul to ruination. To forgive means to forget. However, far too many people on your earth plane claim to forgive those who trespass against them, but they fail to forget about those who trespass against them! Warnings have come and gone over the centuries, but man stubbornly continues to think and act his way, assuming his laws are wise, just, and fair. No. Man's laws have created havoc, pain, and suffering throughout time immemorial simply because he is too stubborn to harmonize in life, to live in peace, and to heed God's Laws.

I tell you, Manuana, everlasting peace is coming to planet Earth, an Earth that will be evil-free!

What are the Universal Cosmic Laws, Oscar?

Earth has ten of them assigned to it many centuries ago! These Holy Rules were and continue to be the Universal Cosmic Laws of God. Nothing can be added or subtracted from these Commandment Laws, and, of course, it is up to each individual person on your earth plane to adhere to and follow these Laws simply, wisely, and logically! There are many countries on your earth plane today which strongly undermine and oppose the Wisdom and Power of God, basing their earthbound wisdom on pride, selfishness, and satanic-rooted, warlike principles and suppressions. When man harms man in any manner, then he is working against God and His Cosmic Laws. My sincerest advice to anyone who adheres to anti-God concepts and actions is to change now. There is still time to do so!

Oscar, how vast is Earth's universe?

Manuana, there are countless universes beyond Earth's. Your universe and solar system are considered small in size as compared to others within the infinite Universal Cosmos. The vast majority of habitable solar systems within a universe consist of one or two suns and twelve planets of which usually three are habitable, but there are exceptions to this rule. Each habitable planet has one or more moons and can be larger or smaller than Earth. There are ancient and present day intergalactic bases scattered throughout your universe. You could multiply each individual species of insect on your earth plane by ten hundred billion to give you some brief idea as to approximately how many planets beyond your universe actually harbor life. Many habitable planets harbor earth-like people, but many do not! Not all of God's Children look like earth people, nor are these different looking people "humanoid." A "built" robot might be considered humanoid, but no actual creation of life should be placed in this labelled category at any time. Each individual species of created life is unique unto itself, has its own destiny and its own purpose, and will always be known as God's Children!

Earthman's future challenge will be to colonize his own universe, and this he will eventually do!

Before closing the chapters to this book, is there any other "message" you wish to impart, Oscar?

Many people may wonder why all these secrets and hidden treasures are being released and revealed to planet Earth now. Why now? Why were they not released earlier in man's history or perhaps later in man's future? Why you, Manuana, or why me? Is it more practical to assume that God's Wonders to man must simply emanate from a remote past and not from the present or future? Did God ever abandon His Children? No. His Presence was, is, and will continue to be everywhere! You must not shout from the top of a mountain saying, "Hear ye, hear ye, I have a message for you!" No, you will not do this. Peacefully and with love, believe what you have seen and heard, Manuana. Many people on your earth plane may mock, disapprove, or even slur these assigned revelations within this book, but this, I maintain, is highly unimportant and irrelevant. For those who believe, let them believe; for those who disbelieve, let them disbelieve. The time for Earth's "new approaching era" must have its first awakening moment and must have its first awakening hour. Such a time has come. Publish this book throughout Israel (the world) as an assigned gift from Heaven to earth. Be at peace.

Jesus, the King of Light, is coming to earth, and this book is just another humble sign revealing this future event. I know this to be true from this side of life as do millions of others on your earth plane who "sense" His Coming. However, for those who do not believe in Him or in His Coming, this book should serve as a humble cry for a troubled world to stop, to look, and to listen. From this side of life, Manuana, the truth abounds with God and His Wonders, but from your side of life, the world abounds with vast doubts, misconceptions, and "probabilities" about God and His Wonders. Jesus, the King of Light, is coming to earth, when man least expects Him. Be at peace.

In essence, Manuana, you are now placed in a quandary. Is your world ready to listen? This, I maintain, is not your worry! Simply do your best to convey this assigned message to planet Earth. Do your best—for it is love that will survive Earth's hate and trouble, and it is truth and hope that will survive Earth's doubts and indifferences. Be at peace.